T0375292

CALLED AND EQUIPPED

A BIBLE STUDY FOR TEACHERS AND OTHER HARRIED SOULS

KAREN WHEELER

WESTBOW
PRESS®
A DIVISION OF THOMAS NELSON
& ZONDERVAN

WestBow Press books may be ordered through booksellers or by contacting:

WestBow Press
A Division of Thomas Nelson & Zondervan
1663 Liberty Drive
Bloomington, IN 47403
www.westbowpress.com
844-714-3454

All Scriptures are taken from the Holy Bible, NEW INTERNATIONAL VERSION®, NIV® Copyright © 1973, 1978, 1984, 2011 by Biblica, Inc.® Used by permission. All rights reserved worldwide.

ISBN: 979-8-3850-0273-3 (sc)
ISBN: 979-8-3850-0274-0 (e)

Library of Congress Control Number: 2023913122

Print information available on the last page.

WestBow Press rev. date: 09/14/2023

To

All the teachers in my past, who formed me …

All the colleagues and administrators, who journeyed with me …

All the students, from whom I learned …

All the Christian mentors, who showed me the *way* …

To God, Who inspired the blending of all the above into this work.

CONTENTS

WEEK 5: PAUL WAS CALLED

WEEK 6: YOU ARE CALLED

Each of us may be sure that if God sends us over rocky paths, He will provide us with sturdy shoes. He will never send us on any journey without equipping us.

—Alexander Maclaren

(1826–1910)

English pastor of the Union Chapel in Manchester, England

PREFACE

The Middle Ages had a particular form of torture known as the "rack." It's a device on which a person is tied, and at the turn of a crank, they are stretched into submission or confession or whatever the administrator chooses. Today this particular form of torture has evolved into an almost ten-month stint called public-school teaching.

After a welcome-back by your school administrator and a brief visit with your colleagues, you are strapped into staff development, a particularly heinous form of torture that may require large doses of chocolate to remain in some degree of consciousness. The cranking and the stretching begins. How can I possibly go through this again?

Two things are true:

- Teaching is an extremely tough job.
- You just gotta have a sense of humor!

Teaching is not a glamor job. People do not go into teaching to make money. Most people go into teaching because they want to make a difference. They want to touch the future. They want their lives to matter. They feel called.

That, in and of itself, is a noble thing, but too often this call is torpedoed by reality, change, and bureaucracy. Of late, societal pressures of COVID-19, political astigmatism, a strained economy, mental health crises, and even gun violence have piled on more stress so that a career that begins with an honorable calling sometimes sinks into mediocrity, even survival.

Many workers are hopeless, who, having endured cuts after cuts, are doing much more with much less. Left to our own devices, one can endure for only so long, for when hope gets dimmer and dimmer and the negative keeps choking the good, it's hard to arrive fresh and unburdened each morning to face our charges.

The Christian faith is supposed to be practiced beyond Sunday worship, but often Sunday peace and joy are pushed aside and bullied by the anxiety and stress that is so prevalent in workplaces today. *Called and Equipped* was born of a need that was inspired by long, frustrating, and harried days as a teacher navigating the rough seas of public school while trying to maintain some semblance of a faithful Christian in practice.

The enemy is not intent. Most people know the value of study, meditation, and prayer when it comes to strengthening faith. The enemy is time. Carving out a quiet time during a hectic day for reading and contemplation amid the avalanche of the urgent is the hard part.

The vehicle in this study is a teaching environment, but this vehicle can go many places. While it was written from a teacher's perspective, non-teachers have taken the study and have found it to be very easy to apply the principles to their work as well. Everyone has been in a classroom so they can relate to this study and transfer learning to their unique work situation.

Called and Equipped can certainly be a self-study, a go-at-your-own-pace study, but just as worship is enhanced by other believers at church, this study can be more effective when a group of coworkers meet together to discuss and personalize the study. The Bible is all about relationships—first with God and then with other people. Everyone brings to the table a different perspective, so it's good to bounce faith concepts off one another as well. How can these ideas work for my life and our work situation?

While the study was originally designed as a six-week study with five readings per week and then meeting together to discuss that week's reading, it has also been done as a "no homework" study, where everyone comes together and reads through one day's reading and discusses it. As participants become familiar with the rhythm of the study, reading can be done outside of the meeting time, and the pace can be picked up if desired.

The intent is to be "user friendly" to participants while growing a cadre of Christian believers in a work setting to encourage one another. It doesn't take much salt to season a dish. Even a small group of Christians coworkers can flavor a workplace climate and make a job much more palatable.

When you meet, be sure to begin the session by asking God's Holy Spirit to bless and guide your time together. As you discuss questions or comments concerning the material, make sure it is a safe space for everyone. At the end of the session, prayer requests could be raised as the group closes in prayer.

Finally, expect God to work in your life. Expect to begin to see things just a little differently. Be open to change as God leads you.

Dealing with the public has become exhausting. Even when you are a Christian, it is hard, but Christ made promises to His faithful. Matthew 11:28–30 says,

> Come to me, all you who are weary and burdened, and I will give you rest. Take my yoke upon you and learn from me, for I am gentle and humble in heart, and you will find rest for your souls. For my yoke is easy and my burden is light.

If our Christian faith won't work for us in the classroom or in our workplace, it won't work anywhere, and Christ is crucified all over again. As we grieve and wring our hands about the death of our dreams, we *can* open our eyes to see Jesus—resurrected—*alive* and well. Our bitterness and loss *can* turn to joy. Our careers *can* be enriched.

You who feel harried and burdened, come. Come see how God called ordinary folks like you and transformed them into so much more than they could ever ask or imagine. There is one Master Teacher, and He wants to mentor you and be your coworker. He is calling you. Will you come *and let Him equip you?*

Moses Was Called

WEEK 1

Day 1

IS YOUR CALL TO TEACHING
THWARTED AND HALF-HEARTED?

WAS MOSES'S FIRST CALL A WRONG
NUMBER? HELLO ... HELLO ... ?

YOU MADE THE CHOICE A long time ago. It may have been as a child when you loved playing "school," or it may have been because of the teacher who encouraged you and believed in you when no one else did. It could be you really loved your babysitting experiences as a teen, and you knew you had an affinity for kids, or you knew having a family was important to you. And what better place to hone parental skills than in a school?

You didn't choose education because of the money you'd make or the short hours you would work. You didn't go into teaching because of the respect and authority given to teachers today. While having a long summer break may have been attractive, you didn't count on the exhaustive frenzy that occurs before testing or other accountability measures states require. If you're like most students of education, you were drawn into the field of study.

- Take a few minutes to reflect on why you were drawn to the teaching profession.

_____

_____

_____

_____

Moses was drawn to the Israelites. *Read Exodus 1* to understand the environment in which Moses's parents were living. Now *read Exodus 2:1–10* to learn of Moses's birth.

- Instead of joy that Israelites would feel at the birth of a son, they did their best to hide him. Why?

_____

_____

_____

_____

- What did Moses's mother do when she could no longer hide her baby?

_____

_____

_____

Can you just feel the angst Jochebed, Moses's mother, must have felt as she slipped the tar-sealed basket into the water and gave Miriam, Moses's sister, instructions on what to say to the person who drew Moses out of the water? Imagine her joy as Miriam came running to get her mother and how hard it must have been to conceal it as she reached for her hungry son! A bonus to his return was the wages she would receive from the Egyptian princess for caring for Moses.

- In Exodus 2:10, what did the pharaoh's daughter name the baby, and why?

_____

_____

_____

Moses probably did not look like the other little boys in the royal prep school. Perhaps his Egyptian mother told him the story of his adoption to make him feel how special he was to her. Don't you think in the brief time she had him, Moses's Hebrew mother was adamant in her insistence that God's hand was on him to remember his people, the Israelites? In her eyes, it was God's hand that drew him out of the water for a special calling.

So it is likely that Moses grew up thinking he was entitled, different, and called. *Read Exodus 2:11–15* to see how this calling worked out.

- What do you think Moses was feeling as he fled for his life?

_____

_____

_____

- Do you think Moses questioned his call to help his people?

_____

_____

_____

- Did you have a similar experience of frustration and desperation when your call as a new teacher seemed thwarted?

_____

_____

_____

If God's hand was on Moses in such a conspicuous way, then why was he seemingly punished for acting on the call?

OK, in your classroom, what do you do with the smart, feisty little boy who whacks a classmate for their rude behavior toward another student? Would you have sent him to time-out? That's what God did to Moses—sent him to tend sheep for forty years.

Read Exodus 2:16–22. Moses almost got in trouble again by defending Jethro's seven daughters as they watered their flocks, but this time he was rewarded for fighting off the shepherds. After he was invited to eat with them, in the next verse, he was married, and in the following verse, he had begotten a son. Told you he was impetuous!

- If you don't believe Moses was in time-out, catch the name he gave his son in Exodus 2:22 and what it means:

  _____

  _____

  _____

- How do you think Moses was feeling?

  _____

  _____

  _____

- Do you ever feel like you are "residing in a foreign land"?

  _____

  _____

  _____

- Was Moses biding his time? Do you think he felt fulfilled?

  _____

  _____

  _____

- Are you going through the motions? Do you feel fulfilled?

  _____

  _____

  _____

- Are you experiencing a desert season?

  _____

  _____

  _____

Read Ecclesiastes 1:1–14. Do you think forty years of tending sheep would put you in an "Ecclesiastes" frame of mind? This book has Prozac written all over it, doesn't it?

The true authorship of Ecclesiastes is debated by scholars, but it is clearly written from King Solomon's experiences and perspective. While his father, King David, was an ardent follower of God, Solomon was a little too smart for his own britches. Mr. Smarty Pants began his journey as king trying to please God. And God blessed him with great wisdom "to govern (God's) people and to distinguish between right and wrong" (1 Kings 3:9–15). He became too confident in himself and less reliant on God. In his "wisdom," he even began worshipping some of his foreign wives' gods, and Ecclesiastes is an expansion of that wisdom. That's the problem with Ecclesiastes—it's a look at the meaning of life solely through human wisdom.

When you read Ecclesiastes, did you sigh a big sigh and think of your teaching career? Did you think about all the various programs and teaching methods you've used through the years and think (v9) "there is nothing new under the sun"? As (v3, 4) "a generation goes, and a generation comes," "what do people gain from all the toil"?

If you did, then you're probably in the same frame of mind Moses was in as he wandered the deserts of Midian with his flock. Are you wandering with your little flock?

Day 2

MOSES TO THE BURNING BUSH; TEACHER BURNOUT OR BURNING BUSH?

GOD EQUIPS MOSES WITH "STAFF" DEVELOPMENT

*M*UCH LIKE YOU TENDING YOUR classroom flock, Moses was keeping the flock of his father-in-law, Jethro. As you know from shepherding kids, shepherding sheep can be a daunting task, especially in new situations and environments. For Moses, it was like student-teaching, a foretaste of his future career of shepherding the sometimes unruly Israelites.

Moses "led his flock *beyond the wilderness*, and came to Horeb, the mountain of God" (Exodus 3:1).[1] "Beyond the wilderness" suggests being very lost. Do you suppose God drew Moses to Him as he was looking for fresh pasture? Once again, it plays on Moses's name, one who is "drawn out."

Isn't it ironic that Moses's "student flock" went to Horeb as did his Israelite flock much later? He went on a practice run with his student flock. Do you wonder if they had as much difficulty with Moses's leadership as did his Israelite flock later?

Read Exodus 3:1–12. As Moses unknowingly drew near to God, an angel of the Lord spiked his curiosity by setting a bush on fire. When it kept burning and did not burn up, it got Moses's full attention, and God saw this as a teachable moment. "Moses, Moses," God called, riveting Moses's attention. Moses answered his attendance, and God said, "Come no closer! Remove the sandals from your feet, for the place on which you are standing is holy ground." Then God made Himself known as the God of Moses's ancestors and told him He had seen and heard the misery of the Israelites and had come *down* to rescue them and take them to the land He had promised them. Furthermore, "I am sending you to Pharaoh to bring my people, the Israelites out of Egypt." Wow! Moses's first real teaching/shepherding job!

- Can you just imagine Moses telling God, "Wait a minute! I've already tried that. I thought I was called, but it was a disaster!" What makes this calling different?

_____

_____

_____

_____

_____

---

[1] Harper-Collins Study Bible, NRSV.

- Has your calling as a teacher not worked out well? Are you feeling teacher "burn-out"? Can it be a burning bush experience?

  _____

  _____

  _____

Moses *unknowingly* drew near to God, but you must *purposefully* "draw near to God, and He will draw near to you."[2] Is God calling you to stop what you are doing—burning yourself up—and turn to Him? If teacher burnout is your burning bush, then *stop*, turn to God, and listen.

If you are feeling lost, frustrated, overwhelmed, inadequate, *stop right now*—you are standing on holy ground. Take off everything that is keeping you from full contact with God. God is calling your name. He has come down to rescue you from your slavery to these feelings. Right now, answer God—"Here I am" and *listen* to Him!

- What did God say to you when you answered Him?

  _____

  _____

  _____

- Did God assure you as He did Moses, "I will be with you"? What does this assurance mean to you?

  _____

  _____

  _____

- Was Moses completely reassured in *Exodus 3:13*?

  _____

  _____

  _____

No, Moses was not reassured. In fact, Moses kept playing the what-if game. What if they ask me Your name? What if they don't believe me or listen to me but think I am being deceitful? (Exodus 4:1) As humans, we are really good at playing the what-if game. Oswald Chambers says, "We imagine that a little anxiety and worry are an indication of how really wise we are; it is much more an indication of how really wicked we are. Fretting springs from a determination to get our own way ... Fretting is wicked if you are a child of God ... All our fret and worry is caused by calculating without God."[3]

---

[2] James 4:8 NRSV.
[3] Chambers, Oswald. *My Utmost for His Highest.* July 4.

- How did God answer Moses in *Exodus 3:14*?

  _____

  _____

  _____

  _____

- What does "I AM WHO I AM" mean to you?

  _____

  _____

  _____

  _____

Don't you just hate it when your kids argue with you at home or at school? Doesn't it just wear you out? While it may have slipped from its number one rank in the top ten things to say to kids when they argue or question your authority, *because I say so* has, through the ages and in all languages, been a top parental answer to children's incessant questioning. "I AM WHO I AM" is God's "BECAUSE I SAY SO." It's His ultimate argument-stopper.

Moses dutifully listened to God's plan through the rest of Exodus 3, but he just couldn't help himself in Exodus 4:1; he threw in a "but." "But suppose they do not believe me or listen to me," questioned Moses. Don't you just love what God did next? *Read Exodus 4:2–5.* Wouldn't your classroom be a lot easier to manage if you had one of these?

- How did God equip Moses?

  _____

  _____

  _____

- What else did God do to equip Moses in *Exodus 4:6–12*?

  _____

  _____

  _____

  _____

Read Exodus 4:13–17. Surely this final "but" in verse 13 warrants a trip to the principal's office as God's anger mounts.

- What was Moses's final whining plea to God?

  _____

  _____

  _____

- What did God do to appease Moses and get him on his way to Egypt?

_____

_____

_____

OK, multiply Moses's questioning and whining times twenty-two, and you'll know why teachers need a few "staffs" in their classrooms! Wouldn't that be a wonderful "staff development" before school—learning how to use that staff?

On to Egypt with staff in hand!

Teachers save their best lessons, bulletin boards, and teaching tools. As God speaks to you through the lessons in this study, use the space beside the equipment bag to record meaningful statements, ideas, or scriptures you may want to remember and use as He equips you for the task for which He is calling you.

_____

_____

_____

_____

_____

_____

Day 3

MORE BRICKS BUT NO STRAW—
PATIENCE, POISE, AND PERSPECTIVE

HOW CAN WE POSSIBLY DO THIS?

WHAT A TEST FOR THE fledgling leader, Moses, who has spent the last forty years shepherding sheep. Not one of those sheep argued with him or talked back to him—ever! And now he's supposed to shepherd a nation.

First, he has to convince a brother he has never known that despite his Egyptian upbringing, Aaron can trust his Hebrew DNA. Then he has to persuade Aaron to go with him before the most powerful person on earth and tell the pharaoh he must let *all* his Israelite workforce go, a people more numerous than the residents of that land. It would certainly wreak economic disaster for the pyramid-minded Egyptians!

Moreover, God has told Moses that despite the wonders He has taught him to perform, He will harden the pharaoh's resolve to keep the Israelites right where they are (Exodus 4:21–23). Finally, God dictates that Moses threaten to kill the pharaoh's firstborn son. I think any Administration 101 course would discourage that kind of leadership. It was a slow walk back to Egypt!

- Why do you think God would stack the deck so against Moses?

  _____

  _____

  _____

- Have you ever felt as trapped in your circumstances as Moses must have felt?

  _____

  _____

  _____

Amazingly, Aaron did agree to accompany Moses, and when they met with the Israelite elders and showed them the signs God had taught Moses, they believed and worshipped God (Exodus 4:27–31). Whew, one hurdle accomplished! At least the Israelites believed Moses.

Read Exodus 5.

The Israelites' heads had been bowed in worship and praise, and now their heads are bowed low in grief and despair. Just when they thought things couldn't get much worse, they did. They are to make bricks with no straw given to them. They will have to go out and gather straw in addition to the back-breaking brickwork—twice as much work. Some deliverer Moses is!

This is not a new concept in education. Every now and again, and especially of late, budget-crunching includes measures that make the jobs of teachers twice as hard: larger class sizes, smaller budgets, increased duties, reduced resources. Just as the Israelites were thinking, *How can we possibly do this?* educators do this kind of thing all the time.

- What would you as a teacher tell the Israelites about dealing with this impossible task?

_____

_____

_____

_____

- What have you done in the past?

_____

_____

_____

_____

In Exodus 5:22–23, Moses again cried out to the Lord. He had done what God instructed him to do, and yet God had not delivered His people; in fact, He had made their bondage even more devastating!

The Israelites were suffering from "the tyranny of the apparent."[4] What was apparent to the Israelites was that Moses was a liar, their crushing bondage had become even more unbearable, and the Egyptians would certainly kill them. Pastor Dan Johnson says we "must not yield to the pressures of this world and to the tyranny of the apparent. When trouble comes, when God seems to be distant, when prayers seem to be ineffective, when waiting seems unbearable, remember God's saints who cling to God's promise no matter what!" And what promises they are for the Israelites! *Read Exodus 6:1–13.*

- In Exodus 6:6, what three things did God promise the Israelites:

    1_____ 2_____ 3_____

- In Exodus 6:7, what did God promise to do for the Israelites:

_____

_____

_____

_____

---

[4] Johnson, Dan. "God's Faithfulness—Our Patience," *Disciplines*, p. 303, Upper Room, 1992.

- What was the response of the Israelites to God's assurances in Exodus 6:9?

  _____

  _____

  _____

Are you terrorized by the dire situation in so many areas of your life during these tumultuous times? There is upheaval and insecurity on so many fronts: financial, political, educational, medical, relational, spiritual. It has an Ecclesiastes ring to it, doesn't it? Johnson continues his advice, "Patience, poise, and perspective are essential," and "that we rely on God's promise and God's word rather than on what may or may not appear to be results."

- What are some of the promises on which you rely in times of anxiety?

  1.
  2.
  3.

- Have you memorized meaningful scripture to carry you through these times? What are they?

  1.
  2.
  3.

- Think practically: What does *patience* look like in times such as these? (example: list five things you are thankful for each day)

  1.
  2.
  3.

- In practice, what does *poise* look like during this time? (example: set priorities)

  1.
  2.
  3.

- In practice, what does *perspective* look like? (example: daily devotional time)

  1.
  2.
  3.

"Difficulty is actually the atmosphere surrounding a miracle, or a miracle in its initial stage. Yet if it is to be a great miracle, the surrounding condition will be not simply a difficulty but an utter impossibility. And it is the clinging hand of His child that makes a desperate situation a delight to God."[5]

Let the miracles begin!

> When you've done so much with so little for so long,
> you become qualified to do anything with nothing.
> —Anonymous

> Unbelief looks at God through the circumstances,
> just as we often see the sun dimmed by clouds or smoke.
> But faith puts God between itself and its circumstances
> and looks at them through Him.[6]
> —L. B. Cowman

How is God using this lesson to equip you? Record meaningful statements, ideas, and scriptures you may want to remember and use as He equips you for the task for which He is calling you.

_____

_____

_____

_____

_____

_____

_____

---

[5] Cowman, L. B. *Streams in the Desert*, p. 388. October 14.
[6] Cowman, L. B. *Streams in the Desert*, p. 268. July 11.

Day 4

GOLDEN CALF LEADERSHIP

MOSES LEAVES THE CLASSROOM

*T*HE MIRACLES DID COMMENCE, BUT first came the plagues—water to blood, frogs, gnats, flies, diseased livestock, boils, thunder/hail/fire, locusts, darkness—nine, count 'em. Finally, God struck down all the firstborn Egyptian sons and passed over the Hebrew sons: "Because of my mighty hand [Pharaoh] will let them go; because of my mighty hand he will drive them out of his country" (Exodus 6:1).

With each one of the plagues, the Israelites should have been reassured that their God was with them even amidst all the toil and misery they were suffering because of their Egyptian oppressors. Finally, they were "paid" to leave because the Egyptians wanted to get rid of them so badly (Exodus 12:35–36).

Read Exodus 14.

OK, here's where our God just flat showed off! He was trying to impress the Israelites and impress upon them that "He is who He says He is and that He will do what he says He will do."[7] He was trying to cement their belief in Him. The Israelites' fear and despair at the pursuing Egyptian army was washed away as the sea flowed back into its place and wiped out the pharaoh and four hundred years of slavery. God and Moses had, indeed, delivered them and in grand fashion.

They sang songs and celebrated God's might and set out with renewed spirit, but just like some of the students in our classes, the Israelites had a short attention span. They traveled three days and started whining again. God "healed" the water and said if the Israelites listen and obey His commandments, then He would keep them healed as well. Still, they whined and tested God about food (Exodus 16) and water (Exodus 17), but each time God came through for them.

Moses finally got his Hebrew flock to Mount Sinai, where he was given the commission to rescue and shepherd God's people. He had come full circle. Do you think he had that "school's out" frame of mind as he looked forward to a long summer vacation?

Moses did have a long vacation from the Israelites; he went to school with God for forty days and forty nights. Working on his masters in shepherding? No, it's a law degree.

Meanwhile, at the bottom of the hill, the Israelites and Aaron waited. You know the drill … The teacher walks out of the room, and what happens? At first, they work quietly, not knowing when Moses (and God) will be back. Then there's intermittent talking among themselves, followed

---

[7] Moore, Beth. *Believing God.*

by grumbling, which leads to, "He's never coming back! Where are my gold earrings, let's make a cow." Check it out in *Exodus 32:1–26.*

First, what's the matter with you, Aaron? Did you not have a ringside seat to God delivering the Israelites? "Moses said to Aaron, 'What did this people do to you that you have brought so great a sin upon them?'" (Exodus 32:21 NRSV). At which, Aaron replied, "They gave me their gold, I threw it into the fire, and out popped this calf!" Oh, pleeeeease! Can't we expel him, Lord?

We know it was God who worked through Moses and Aaron to allow His will to come to pass; it was not Aaron's own ingenuity. But because Aaron sought approval, his pride swelled into authority and power, and perhaps he welcomed his brother's tardiness and began to set himself up as god. His "success" was actualized as Moses looked down on the mêlée in horror.

Unfortunately, there's a lot of Aaron in most of us. Schools are filled with teacher's pets and folks who seek approval. Most teachers spend their lives placating parents, administrators, and colleagues. Smooth waters are good, but if we are going to get somewhere, we have to paddle, and that makes waves. It's easy for us to say Aaron should have stood up to the Israelites, but then it comes down to the difference between being a peacekeeper and a peacemaker.

- What is a peacekeeper?

  _____

  _____

  _____

- What is a peacemaker?

  _____

  _____

  _____

- Which was Aaron?

  _____

  _____

  _____

- Are you a peacekeeper or a peacemaker at school? At home?

  _____

  _____

  _____

If Aaron had worked to *make* peace with Israelites' unrest instead of bending to them to *keep* the peace and placate them, the situation could have been significantly calmed. What about your life? Is keeping the peace and getting approval your golden calf?

Aaron's pride was fanned into flames as the Israelites looked to him in Moses's absence.

Maybe, in his heart of hearts, he was tired of playing "second fiddle," and he welcomed their dependence and confidence in him. Oswald Chambers says, "Pride is the deification of self,"[8] and that's exactly what Aaron did. He readily came up with the plan for the golden calf, for according to scripture, he didn't even hesitate or mull over consulting God.

Are there times in your life when you foster the dependence and confidence of others to build yourself up? Pride says, "I'm only helping," but pride, even as subtle as this, has a way of flaring up, and if left unchecked, pride can destroy the give and take balance of relationships.

How do you check pride? Henry and Richard Blackaby have a great assessment: "[Pride] hinders you from doing what brings glory to God."[9] Conversely, if what you are doing does not bring glory to God, then it's probably pride. Could pride be your golden calf?

It wasn't only Aaron's pride that got him into trouble, it was his style of authority as well. As Moses's backup man, it was natural for the Israelites to turn to him. Teachers are natural authority figures too; in classrooms, in team meetings, campus committees, even district-wide panels, teachers consult with and advise others on a daily basis. Outside of school, you can nearly always tell when a teacher is present because they are such "take charge" personality types.

God spent forty years molding Moses into the leader He wanted, but Aaron clearly did not have the training in patience and humility.

- Can you think of an example where a prideful, defensive approach yielded harmful results in a school/work environment?

  _____
  _____
  _____

- How could this situation have had a more desirable outcome if patience and humility had been employed with authority?

  _____
  _____
  _____

Are patience and humility part of your authority persona, or is defensive authority your golden calf?

Of course, the huge difference between Moses and Aaron was that Moses had a relationship with God. Moses depended on God to lead him. Even when Moses was called by God to lead the Israelites out of Egypt, Moses, in his humility, didn't want that call, but God promised Moses He would be there for him every step of the way. Aaron didn't have that dependence on God. He was ready to take the reins, he jumped at the chance, but he clearly had no idea where to go, and he very much led them astray.

Aaron's peacekeeping, prideful "Because I say so" style of leadership (leadership *without* God)

---

[8] Chambers, Oswald. *My Utmost for His Highest,* p. 119.

[9] Blackaby, Henry and Richard. *Experiencing God Day by Day*, p. 186.

produced a golden calf. Moses's peacemaking, humble "Because I AM says so" mode of authority (leadership with God in control) produced miracles.

How will you lead?

It's a simple equation:

Aaron x (peacekeeping + pride + defensive authority) - God = idolatry
Moses x (peacemaking + humility + patient authority) + God = miracles

How is God using this lesson to equip you? Record meaningful statements, ideas, and scriptures you may want to remember and use as He equips you for the task for which He is calling you.

_____

_____

_____

_____

_____

_____

_____

Day 5

Stiff Necks Eased by the *Heart* Principles

Moses Tries to Rein a Stiff-Necked People

*A*s a puppy, he was easy to train and very attentive to the one who held the leash, so the small collar worked fine. When he got bigger and more confident, his curiosity and distractibility prevailed over the leash and the one who was trying to direct his path.

This was extremely evident one morning as they were walking past a garbage truck and its oh-so-irresistible aroma. Beau's owner recognized the enticement, but it was a split second too late, for as he took off, so did her legs beneath her. Screaming from a belly-buster position on the grass, she looked up to see a man in coveralls who could now qualify for the US Olympic track team perched atop his truck.

At the recommendation of the folks at the pet store, Beau got a pinch or prong collar. Now when he starts off course from the walk, the collar pinches in, and the prongs easily convince him he needs to stay put. Before the change in collars, Beau was very stiff-necked, very hard to guide and direct, extremely hard to take for a walk.

Pinch collars were invented a few centuries too late to help poor Moses and his forty-year walk with the Israelites. Even God complained to Moses, "I have seen this people, how stiff-necked they are." After the Israelites "ran after" the golden calf with Moses in "belly-buster position on the grass," God further says, "Now let me alone, so that my wrath may burn hot against them and I may consume them; and of you [Moses] I will make a great nation" (Exodus 32:9–10[10]). Even God gets irritated with stubborn people.

Make no mistake, we are not talking about tenacity or the perseverance side of stubborn; we are talking about the pigheaded, "cut-off-your-nose-to-spite-your-face" kind of stubborn. We are not talking about stubborn belief in God; we are talking about the "I can't believe they don't get it, they're only hurting themselves" kind of stubborn.

Deuteronomy 9 is a recap of Israelite rebelliousness and a major "chewing out" for all their disobedience during their wilderness years.

---

[10] Harper-Collins Study Bible, NRSV.

- After the Israelites "ran after" the golden calf, what position did Moses assume in *Deuteronomy 9:18*?

  _____

  _____

  _____

It was the same position as Beau's owner found herself when he got away from her.

- In *Deuteronomy 10:12–13*, Moses summarized the covenant. What are the five things the Lord requires of Israel?

  1) To _____ 2) To _____

  3) To _____ 4) To _____

  5) To _____

- In the above passage, why does the Lord require these things of Israel?

  _____

  _____

  _____

- Generations later, God recounted to *Jeremiah* in *7:22–26* how disobedient and "stiff-necked" the Israelites were during the exodus from Egypt and up to the time of Jeremiah. Why was God so adamant about their obedience in 7:23?

  _____

  _____

  _____

The Bible has twenty-eight references to some variation of the word "stubborn," which includes nineteen references to "stiff-necked" alone.[11] Our stubbornness is a huge disappointment to our Father who longs to care for us. In 2 Chronicles 30:8, it says, "Do not be stiff-necked, as your fathers were; submit to the Lord." That's the part that is so hard for us—submitting our will to God's will.

You've seen stubbornness. It is in your classroom, in your team meetings, in the parents' group, and perhaps in your own household. It could even be looking back at you in the bathroom mirror. It's our human condition, our wanting to "do our own thing," but God loves us too much to let us stray. He is protective when it comes to His children.

If you are feeling the pinch of God trying to lead you in some area of your life, stop and submit to the only One who can perfectly guide you. He knows the path; He knows what's ahead. He

---

[11] What Does the Bible Say About Stubbornness? | eHow.com http://www.ehow.com/about_4587766_what-does-bible-say-stubbornness.html#ixzz1Sha0Tjdj.

especially knows the pitfalls away from the path. Take time to pray for Him to soften your stiff will and make you more sensitive to His lead. Give Him the reins of your life.

Once your heart is reined in by your loving Father, then you are prepared to deal with those other stubborn people in your life. If we are going to "live from the heart" of God, "we must become aware of the needs of those around us" and how God wants us to answer those needs. This is the premise of the HEART Principles designed by Minister Roy Trueblood in his Partners in Ministry curriculum.[12]

Trueblood believes we all "thirst" for five things in the form of unspoken requests:

> **H**ear and understand me.
> **E**ven if you disagree, please don't make me wrong.
> **A**cknowledge the greatness within me.
> **R**emember to look for my loving intentions.
> **T**ell me the truth with compassion.

Everyone is texting, twittering, tweeting, and blogging, but is anyone listening, or are we just "tower of babbling"? We all desire to be heard, and this first HEART Principle, *Hear and understand me*, focuses on *active listening*. You know how most people listen—only halfway listening while they are planning the next thing they are going to say. According to Trueblood, listening for understanding is an act of caring.

Active listening may include listening-checks or paraphrasing conversation to make sure the message you've received is right. Ask questions to understand their frame of reference—where they're coming from. Listen for what they are saying, but also listen for what they aren't saying—their insecurities and their unspoken fears. Perhaps use a summary statement to show that you have listened to them and really heard what they have said. Put your defenses aside and listen, for only then will we begin to understand.

Even if you disagree, please don't make me wrong. "We must learn to separate people from their ideas," states Trueblood. It's OK to disagree with what they are saying, but don't agree to disrespect them as a person by making them wrong. Don't make the cost of winning an argument losing a friend or colleague.

The third request from the heart is *acknowledge the greatness within me*. We are children of God, and that, in itself, is enough to celebrate and affirm in others. We look for ways to encourage and inspire students, but no one outgrows the need for recognition and appreciation. In fact, we, as adults, get beaten down by life occasionally, and a little affirmation can sooth and ease one who is stiff-necked.

Remember to look for my loving intentions. We are "to give others the benefit of the doubt, to look for positive motives before becoming overly critical ... Living from the heart means looking for loving intentions before we jump to conclusions," declares Trueblood.

Finally, *tell me the truth with compassion*. So often a trait or characteristic that irritates us in others is the very thing we are blind to in ourselves. It's very hard to hear and to accept that truth,

---

[12] Roy Trueblood, Partners in Ministry curriculum, The HEART Principles.

but if it is delivered in a loving, compassionate way, the Spirit of God in us will receive it and help us to deal with it. Likewise, when there is need to approach others with a truth they might not want to hear, pray for the situation and for the words God would have you use to speak the truth with His compassion.

These HEART Principles aren't easy, and they aren't natural. That's one clear indication they are God's ways. "For my thoughts are not your thoughts, nor are your ways my ways, says the Lord. For as the heavens are higher than the earth, so are my ways higher than your ways and my thoughts than your thoughts" (Isaiah 55:8–9).

Moses was an ordinary man who God took for an extraordinary journey that began with a call, a call to relationship with Him. Moses yielded his will to God, and God led him every step of the way. You are called—are you yielded to God?

How is God using this lesson to equip you? Record meaningful statements, ideas, and scriptures you may want to remember and use as He equips you for the task for which he is calling you.

_____

_____

_____

_____

_____

_____

GROUP QUESTIONS FOR MOSES WAS CALLED

- Can you relate to Moses' frustration when his call was thwarted?

- What are some of the factors in school/work that make you feel like you're in a foreign land or a desert?

- Moses was definitely feeling overwhelmed and stepped out in faith with God. What are some things you do when you are feeling overwhelmed at school/work?

- Share some of your answers from Moses Day 3 to the ways you practice patience, poise, and perspective.

- Respecting your zeal for excellence in meeting God's call, how can you keep teaching from becoming your golden calf?

- How might the equations at the end of Day 4's reading help you?

- Discuss the HEART Principles and give some possible applications in the school/ work setting.

David Was Called

WEEK 2

Day 1

DAVID HAD A HEART FOR GOD; WHERE'S YOUR HEART?

DAVID, THE UNLIKELY, WAS CALLED; WOULD YOU HAVE CALLED ON DAVID?

*D*AVID WAS THE YOUNG BOY we would all want to be in our classroom. He was a smart, fine-looking, outdoorsy youngster, dressed in a worn, dusty hand-me-down tunic. But you couldn't seat him just anyplace in your classroom; he would need to sit near a window because of the distinct ovine aroma and away from the girls, for despite the strong scent, girls seemed to be attracted to him and vice versa. Why would God choose him to be anointed king? *Read 1 Samuel 16:1–13.*

- Why did the Lord choose David to be anointed king?

_____

_____

_____

What was it about the heart of this young man that the King of Creation would be willing to hand him the reins of His chosen people? Could we have looked into David's eyes and seen greatness? Before we read more about the young man, David, let's look at the situation into which he was thrust.

After the leadership of Moses and Joshua, God raised up for Israel judges as needed. The Bible speaks of twelve judges and then goes into the story of Samuel, who is called a prophet and the last Hebrew judge. In 1 Samuel 12:12–15, Samuel addressed the Israelites and told them that God had been faithful to them all these years and had raised up leaders; however, the Israelites kept clamoring for a king, so God had Samuel anoint Saul as king. In Hebrew, Saul means "asked for."[13] He warned them in verses 14–15, "If you fear the Lord and serve and obey him and do not rebel against his commands, and if both you and the king who reigns over you follow the Lord your God—good! But if you do not obey the Lord, and if you rebel against his commands, his hand will be against you as it was against your fathers."

In 1 Samuel 13, Saul called up the Israelites to fight the Philistines, and as the enemy army amassed, the soldiers who were with Saul were terrified and began to scatter. Although he was

---

[13] Moore, Beth. *David—Seeking a Heart Like His*. Video session 1.

supposed to wait for Samuel to sacrifice burned offerings, arrogant Saul went ahead and offered up the burned offerings himself. Samuel rebuked him and prophesied, "The Lord has sought out a man after his own heart and appointed him leader of his people, because you have not kept the Lord's command."

King Saul already had one strike against him when Samuel, in 1 Samuel 15, conveyed to him a message from the Lord: Go destroy the Amalekites because of their raids against the Israelites when they were wandering with Moses in the wilderness. When he went against the Amalekites, his army destroyed everything but the best livestock and Agag, king of the Amalekites. Again, he disobeyed the Lord's distinct order; he did not destroy everything. As Saul argued with Samuel that he had obeyed—he was simply saving the best livestock to sacrifice to God—Samuel responded, "To obey is better than sacrifice, and to heed is better than the fat of rams. For rebellion is like the sin of divination, and arrogance like the evil of idolatry. Because you have rejected the word of the Lord, he has rejected you as king" (1 Samuel 15:22–23).

Beth Moore, in her study, *David—Seeking a Heart Like His*,[14] says Saul's fatal flaw was that his "position exceeded his passion for the job. His job was bigger than his heart. A great leader … leads with his head and his heart." Moore goes on to say that Saul tried to appease God, and "there's a big difference between appeasing God and pleasing God."

Do a heart-check. Is your passion, your heart still in your teaching job? Are you a new teacher who is overwhelmed by your position? Maybe you need a wise "Samuel" to guide you. Perhaps you are having a huge issue outside of school that is sucking the passion to teach right out of you, and you are struggling to do the job you really want to do. If you have many years of teaching experience and know how to "cut corners," are you appeasing or pleasing God? Has your passion for teaching faded?

- What are your thoughts?

  _____

  _____

  _____

God knows where your heart is. Seek Him; listen to Him. Let Him help you find the joy of pleasing Him, and in doing so, your passion may return. If not, maybe He's preparing you for other work in which to glorify Him.

God knew David's heart, so let's go on with his story by *reading 1 Samuel 16:14–23*.

- What more do we know about David from the reading?

  _____

  _____

  _____

---

[14] Moore, Beth. *David—Seeking a Heart Like His*. Video session 1.

Perhaps young David spent his time in the pasture watching the sheep while teaching himself how to play the harp, which, according to *The Revell Bible Dictionary,*[15] is actually a handheld stringed instrument called a lyre. Besides being an accomplished musician, David was respectful, articulate, brave, and confident enough to enter Saul's service as the "royal doldrums banisher" and armor-bearer. How ironic, the Spirit of the Lord had departed from Saul, and when an evil spirit tormented him, the only person who could comfort Saul was the one on whom God had placed His Spirit and had anointed to take his place, David.

Isn't it amazing how God used shepherding to train David to lead a nation, much as He did Moses? Through shepherding, David learned to watch his whole flock while keeping a compassionate eye on the special needs of the stragglers—the older sheep and the lambs. He had to learn to find good pasture and water while watching for predators. At times he had to defend his flock, so he developed the skills and heart of a warrior. He had lots of time to practice with his slingshot with plenty of time left to work out the sour notes on his lyre. All the while, God was watching him and shaping his heart.

David was again tending the sheep when his father told him to take food to his brothers who were with King Saul and the Israelite army facing the Philistines. *Read 1 Samuel 17:20–28.*

- Why do you think David's oldest brother, Eliab, was so angry?

  _____

  _____

  _____

Eliab had some extremely strong words to say to David. Could it be that at the heart of his anger was fear, and as the eldest brother, he was responsible for David's safety while he was there? He certainly did a good job of trying to shame him back to the flock, only David knew something Eliab didn't know. *Read 1 Samuel 17:29–37* to discover what it was.

"David said to Saul, 'Let no one lose heart on account of this Philistine; your servant will go and fight him'" (1 Samuel 17:32).

- What was it that David knew in his heart that gave him the confidence Eliab interpreted as conceit?

  _____

  _____

  _____

Read 1 Samuel 17:38–50, the story of David and Goliath, with new eyes and savor the story.

J. Daniel Hayes[16] suggests that the Goliath story demonstrated Saul's inability or unwillingness to be king and lead the Israelites, which corroborates Beth Moore's theory that Saul's "position

---

[15] *The Revell Bible Dictionary,* p. 468.

[16] J. Daniel Hayes, "Reconsidering the Height of Goliath," *Journal of the Evangelical Theological Society* 48/4 (December 2005) 701-14 (available online as a pdf file).

exceeded his passion." Hayes further compared Saul to Goliath: Saul was a big man, probably a head taller than most Israelites, and his armor and weapons were comparable to Goliath's. But while David is ready to go into battle with a slingshot and five stones, "[Saul] has been cowering in fear instead of rising up and attacking the threat to his sheep [Israel]."

Somewhere on those hills, leading and following sheep, David developed his strongest attribute: a personal rock-solid relationship with his Lord. God knew David's heart, and David knew and reverenced the heart of God. As you prepare to go into the battle of each day, are you armed with and secured in God? Or are you cowering in fear of what the day will bring?

If you looked deep into the eyes of the shepherd boy, David, would you have seen greatness? What would young David see if he looked back into your eyes?

How is God using this lesson to equip you? Record meaningful statements, ideas, and scriptures you may want to remember and use as He equips you for the task for which He is calling you.

Day 2

WHEN YOU'RE CHASED BY INJUSTICE, TO WHOM DO YOU TURN?

DAVID IS CHASED BY IRRATIONAL SAUL; ARE YOU BEING CHASED BY INJUSTICE?

*A*S WITH MOST CASES OF fame and fortune, there are positive and negative features. Successful Hollywood and sports types usually enjoy all the perks of accomplishment and fame, but they will bemoan the loss of their privacy. The young shepherd David was catapulted into fame when Goliath hit the ground, and life, as he knew it, would never be the same.

As Saul and his men paraded through towns after the giant was killed, they were met by women who were "singing and dancing, with joyful songs and with tambourines and lutes. As they danced, they sang: 'Saul has slain his thousands, and David his tens of thousands'" (1 Samuel 18:6–7).

Oops. They couldn't have just hummed the tune or put it on mute as Saul passed by? No, he heard every word, and the celebratory song was a match that landed on the fireworks stand of Saul's insecurity. From that moment forth, "Saul kept a jealous eye on David" (1 Samuel 18:8–9). And from that moment on, Saul seesawed between sanity and madness.

Read what happened the very next day between Saul and David in *1 Samuel 18:10–11*. Do you wonder why Saul would be listening to music with a spear in his hand? Are you thinking maybe once would have been enough for you to dodge the spear before you would have developed a plan B? "Pin the spear on David" was Saul's parlor game that day, but in a moment of lucidity, Saul's fear of him drove him to send David away to battle, hoping David would be killed.

Of course, this plan backfired on Saul too, for "all Israel and Judah loved David, because he led them in their [successful] campaigns" (1 Samuel 18:16). Still, Saul tried again by promising David his daughter in marriage for the price of one hundred Philistine foreskins. Saul just knew that would get him killed, but ever-resourceful David "presented" two hundred foreskins to King Saul for his daughter Michal (1 Samuel 18:24–27).

Finally, in 1 Samuel 19:9–10, Saul again tried to "pin the spear on David," while David was playing the harp, and the spear drove into the wall as nimble David escaped. "That night David made good his escape."

- Why do you think David stuck around so long without running away?

_____

_____

- Do you ever feel like you are dodging spears in your job? How?

_____

_____

_____

One reason David stuck around was because of Jonathan, his best friend. Right after David killed Goliath, "Jonathan became one in spirit with David, and he loved him as himself"; in fact, "Jonathan made a covenant with David" because of his love for him and gave him his own robe and tunic and his implements of protection—his sword, bow, and his belt (1 Samuel 18:1–4). There was a test of that friendship in 1 Samuel 19:1–7, when Saul told Jonathan and everyone around him to kill David. After Jonathan warned David, he spoke to his father and reminded him of all the good David had done for Saul and all of Israel. He asked him why he would want to kill an innocent man. Of course, Saul had no reason to kill David other than the fact that he was insanely jealous of him. So after a time in battle with the Philistines, triumphant David came back to Saul's house and again played the harp. That's when Saul redecorated his wall by planting his spear into it as David barely missed becoming a pinup.

David went to his house under the watchful eye of Saul's men, and with the help of his wife, Michal, Saul's daughter, he escaped out the window and ran to Samuel. The Lord had an interesting way of intervening and protecting David in 1 Samuel 19:18–24. As Saul's men, intent upon capturing David, came upon Samuel and his prophets prophesying, they also began prophesying. Saul sent another group of captors and a third group who all were overtaken by prophesying. Finally, Saul came and "stripped off his robes and also prophesied in Samuel's presence," and "he lay that way all that day and night."

David again escaped and went to Jonathan, and their interchange in 1 Samuel 20 is very much two best friends trying to figure out a difficult situation together. Jonathan can't quite wrap his mind around his father's hatred of David, and together, they came up with a plan to test Saul's intentions toward David. _Read 1 Samuel 20:12–17._

- In verse 15, what does Jonathan request of David that may have impacted David's treatment of Saul later?

_____

_____

_____

When Jonathan put their plan into effect, Saul's intention concerning David soon became clear. _Read 1 Samuel 20:30–34 and 41–42._

- In verse 31, Saul gives a reason why he wanted David dead. What was that reason?

_____

_____

_____

- Have you ever experienced the grief Jonathan experienced when two people you love are hostile?

_____

_____

_____

As they parted, both of their hearts were broken. Can you just imagine how "alone" David felt? He had run to Samuel and then to Jonathan, and neither of them could provide shelter or solace for David. He was alone.

Have you ever been alone like that? Have you ever been alone in a hospital room late at night with a loved one who may not live until morning? Have you ever been alone the first night after your spouse told you s/he wanted a divorce and left? When the darkness seems to wrap around your soul, when you struggle to breathe because of the crushing heaviness of your heart, when the nighttime of your fear seems to swallow you whole, there is One who is there with you.

It is in this place that we discover if God is our God. If we seek solace from other people or from a bottle or from a shopping spree or a bank account in these moments, then our god has a little "g." Our training wheels are off. Either we keep peddling right into the arms of our Father God or we will come tumbling down.

When David was in this place, *read* how he handled it in *Psalm 142*.

According to Beth Moore,[17] here, David shows us how to handle our anguish: (1) David prayed. (2) David cried aloud. (3) He poured out his complaint to God. (4) He rehearsed his trust in God. (5) He longed for God's presence. (6) David confessed his desperate need. Moore adds, "I am convinced this is one of the major contributors to David's Godlike heart: He viewed his heart as a pitcher, and he poured everything in it on his God, whether it was joy or sadness, bitterness or fear … Feelings can be a little like our laundry. Sometimes we can't sort them until we dump them on the table."

God cemented his relationship with David during those lonely times as David's character was tested, and David tested God's character as well. *God Calling*[18] speaks of a Divine Friend and says,

> Have you ever realized the wonder of the friendship you can have with Me? Have you ever thought what it means to be able to summon at will the God of the World? Even with a privileged visitor to an earthly king there is the palace ante-chamber, and the time must be at the pleasure of the king. But to My subjects I have given the right to enter My Presence when you will, nay more they can summon Me to bedside, to workshop [to classroom]—and I am there. Could Divine Love do more? Your nearest earthly friend cannot be with you on the instant. Your Lord, your Master, your Divine Friend—Yes.

From a cave, David cried out to his Divine Friend in Psalm 142, and God met David there, sustained him, and strengthened him to go on. "Could Divine love do more?"

---

[17] Moore, Beth. *David: Seeking a Heart Like His*, pp. 61–62.
[18] *God Calling*. June 25.

David's hope and strength were renewed, and twice,[19] when bitterness and anger could have snuffed the life out of Saul by David's hand, he refused to let those emotions sway him. Saul was God's anointed, and David's love for God and his love for his friend Jonathan bound up the cry for justice and let mercy fall from his hand instead. Mercy was, indeed, enthroned in the heart of this king, David.

What about you? When you feel the spear of injustice whiz past you, do you cry out to God? When your mentors and closest friends don't have the answers or can't be there for you and you're absolutely alone in your distress, do you pour out your heart to your Divine Friend? Do you hold on to Him until His light breaks the strangle hold of your darkness and your trembling heart beats stronger with hope? Can you release bitterness and frustration from your heart and let mercy rain down instead?

The quality of mercy is not strained.
It droppeth as the gentle rain from heaven
Upon the place beneath. It is twice blest:
It blesseth him that gives and him that takes.
Tis mightiest in the mightiest; it becomes
The throned monarch better than his crown.
His scepter shows the force of temporal power,
The attribute to awe and majesty,
Wherein doth sit the dread and fear of kings.
But mercy is above this sceptered sway;
It is enthroned in the hearts of kings;
It is an attribute of God himself;
And earthly power doth then show like God's
When mercy seasons justice.[20]

How is God using this lesson to equip you? Record meaningful statements, ideas, and scriptures you may want to remember and use as He equips you for the task for which He is calling you.

_____

_____

_____

_____

_____

_____

_____

---

[19] 1 Samuel 24 and 1 Samuel 26.
[20] Shakespeare, William. *The Merchant of Venice.* http://www/bardwev/net/content/readings/merchant/lines.

Day 3

Six Qualities of Excellent Leadership

David Leads His Ragtag Band; How Is Your Little Band Faring?

During the 1960s there was a very popular television series called *The Fugitive*. It's the story of Dr. Richard Kimble, who was wrongly convicted of killing his wife and escaped on his way to death row. For 120 episodes, Kimble was a man on the run, constantly changing locations and identities in order to find the real killer, while continually escaping the obsessed police lieutenant, whose charge was to recapture him. Coincidentally, the actor's real name was David, David Janssen.

Our David was also a fugitive, and as a hunted man, he hid. In 1 Samuel 22:1–2, it tells us he "escaped to the cave of Adullam," and "All those who were in distress or in debt or discontented gathered around him, and he became their leader. About four hundred men were with him." The *HarperCollins Study Bible* says, "David, now a fugitive from Saul's justice, becomes the champion and leader of everyone in the region who is disfranchised, disenchanted, and embittered."

Scripture doesn't say they are murderers, thieves, lepers, or mentally ill. We're talking about the same kinds of people your principal stands before in a staff meeting. We're talking about folks on your team, even kids in your classroom. We're talking about those who don't feel that they belong; those whose "happily ever after" lay in ashes; those who fell upon some hard times and had no support; those who are weary of society's pretense and hypocrisy; those who, at the root of their eternal bad mood and disgruntlement, fear.

Here again, we have a glimpse of God's sense of humor: "OK, David, if you are going to be king of Israel, let's see how you do with these four hundred," which soon swelled to six hundred in the next chapter. Battle-tested David had killed a lion, a bear, and a giant, but would he be able to shepherd this flock? How does he do it?

One thing a good leader has to do is to be willing to accept responsibility, especially when his decision has hurt people or caused negative fallout. In 1 Samuel 21, David went to Nob to the priest Ahimelech and asked for food and a weapon. Unaware that David was on the run, Ahimelech helped David, and later he was slaughtered for doing so by Saul's man, Doeg, along with eighty-four other priests and every living thing in the city of Nob. Abiathar, one of Ahimelech's sons, escaped and fled to David and told him what happened. David said, "I am responsible for the death of your father's whole family. Stay with me; don't be afraid; the man who is seeking your life is seeking mine also. You will be safe with me" (1 Samuel 22:22–23). David not only accepted responsibility, but he also shepherded the one he had wronged.

- Can you think of an example of good leadership, perhaps in school, in which the leader accepted responsibility for a negative outcome and "shepherded" the situation?

_____

_____

_____

A second characteristic of good leadership is integrity, leading by example. In 1 Samuel 24, David's men encouraged him to kill Saul. David was tempted to exact revenge but was "conscience-stricken" after cutting off the corner of Saul's robe. Two chapters later, in 1 Samuel 26, Abishai requested to kill sleeping Saul, and David answered, "Don't destroy him! Who can lay a hand on the Lord's anointed and be guiltless? As surely as the Lord lives … the Lord himself will strike him; either his time will come and he will die, or he will go into battle and perish." Perhaps, in the first incident, David was tempted to exact justice, but in the second opportunity, he demonstrated his complete trust that God would take care of Saul, even if it meant an indefinite delay for his reign as king. His integrity and his restraint spoke volumes to his men.

- Have you ever experienced having to restrain yourself when you are tempted to disrespect or "strike back" at one who is in a leadership position over you?

_____

_____

_____

- Have you ever considered your refusal to disrespect them as a way of honoring God?

_____

_____

_____

In 1 Samuel 25, David "shepherded his men to green pastures" by looking out for their welfare, another mark of good leadership. Nabal, was a rich man, a descendant of the Exodus hero, Caleb, who lived in Carmel with his wife, Abigail. David learned Nabal was shearing sheep, a time of work and feasting, so he sent ten of his young men to ask for food since David and his men had been out in the field with his shepherds and had protected them. When Nabal flatly turned them down, David was angry because of the disrespect of Nabal to his men and to him. It was an insult for Nabal not to feed them, so David set out to avenge his men. The wisdom and humility of Abigail saved her husband as she gathered food and brought it to David who had acted to provide for his men.

As we travel on with David and his men, we see a fourth quality of leadership: wisdom. In 1 Samuel 27, David decided to leave Saul and Judah and "enter the service" of the king of Gath, in Philistine territory. Achish gave him a country town, Ziklag, so David and his six hundred men and all their families relocated there. Here, "David deludes Achish by pretending to raid and plunder Israel and its allies while really fighting against Israel's enemies."[21] Instead of being disloyal to Israel, he very much remained loyal while jointly winning the confidence of an enemy of Israel. His wisdom yielded him a "win-win" situation and cemented the loyalty of his men to him as well.

David again demonstrated the wisdom needed by a good leader in 1 Samuel 30. After the Philistines wisely sent David and his men home when they gathered to fight Israel, David and his men discovered the Amalekites had raided and burned their home city, Ziklag, and had taken their families captive. They wept and grieved, and in their grief, the men spoke of stoning David (1 Samuel 30:6), "But David found strength in the Lord his God." David's leadership was not based on emotions; he wisely sought the One who is all-wise. David asked the Lord for direction, and God assured them they would "succeed in the rescue."

- In the midst of an emotional crisis, have you sought the Lord's wisdom? How did He strengthen you and give you wisdom to deal with it?

  _____

  _____

  _____

David wisely and humbly called on God, for he knew if it were God's fight and His will, He would also provide victory. The battle may not be easy or quick, but victory was assured. Beth Moore adds, "We cannot pick fights or choose our own battles and expect God to get involved and fight for us. But when God ordains or permits our battles to be used to accomplish a divine end and we depend on God through every sweep of our sword, we will grow stronger instead of weaker."[22]

After David and his men found and fought the Amalekites and recovered their families and belongings, we see another characteristic of great leadership: fairness. Two hundred of David's men had been too exhausted to pursue the Amalekites, so they were left beside a ravine with the supplies. When the four hundred came back with their families and all the plunder they had recovered, some of the "troublemakers" told those who had stayed they could have their families but none of the plunder. David would have none of that. "David replied, 'No, my brothers, you must not do that with what the Lord has given us. He has protected us and handed over to us the forces that came against us … The share of the man who stayed with the supplies is to be the same as that of him who went down to the battle. All will share alike'" (1 Samuel 30:23–24).

- What are some ways you lead your class to understand fairness?

  _____

  _____

  _____

---

[21] *HarperCollins Study Bible*, p. 460.
[22] Moore, Beth. *David: Seeking a Heart Like His*, p. 111.

A sixth characteristic of great leadership is compassion, which David demonstrated in 2 Samuel 9, when he located Jonathan's son, Mephibosheth. David had vowed to show kindness to Jonathan's family (1 Samuel 20:15), and despite the fact Mephibosheth was crippled, thus making him a societal outcast, David restored his inheritance and made him a member of his own family.

- How do you help the children in your classroom learn to accept and not belittle others who struggle outside of the norm of other children?

_____

_____

_____

The mark of a civilized nation is its capacity to care for the disadvantaged, the disenfranchised, and the disabled. That's precisely what God had in mind when He spent approximately fifteen years, from the time of Samuel's anointing until becoming king over Israel, honing these leadership skills into David. The fact that David took his ragtag army from the cave of Adullam to the throne in Jerusalem was proof of his outstanding and godly leadership skills. The six leadership skills were all sheathed in a humble shepherd boy who had the audacity to believe that his God would shepherd him, "The Lord is my shepherd …"[23]

How is God using this lesson to equip you? Record meaningful statements, ideas, and scriptures you may want to remember and use as He equips you for the task for which He is calling you.

_____

_____

_____

_____

_____

_____

---

[23] Psalm 23:1.

Day 4

DISTINGUISHING BETWEEN OUR WANTS AND OUR NEEDS

DAVID SUCCUMBS TO TEMPTATION; WHAT FUELS OUR DISCONTENT?

*H*OW OFTEN WE HAVE HEARD it: An honorable man who is at the top of his profession succumbs to temptation and is disgraced. It's happened to CEOs, athletes, politicians, pastors, and presidents, and while we aren't nearly as hard on the CEOs and athletes, those who hold our esteem and trust put cracks in our innocence, and cynicism begins to ooze out, along with tons of fodder for jokes on late-night television.

In Day 3, we extoled the virtues of David's leadership of his band of misfits, and somewhere along the way, David and his warriors, under God's direction, became a force to reckon with. Roughly twenty-three years after Samuel anointed David, he became King of Israel and Judah. "David defeated Israel's enemies, expanded the nations' borders, and established Jerusalem as its political and religious center. His military, political, and religious innovations initiated Israel's golden age, and unified the Hebrew people as never before."[24] At a pinnacle when things could not be going any better, the fall began. What is it about success that puts us on the fast track to a train wreck?

Henry and Richard Blackaby reflect, "It is sometimes easier to handle poverty or weakness than wealth or strength. Poverty causes us to recognize our need for God. Prosperity persuades us that we no longer require Him."[25] We do not know David's state of mind, but we do know that "In the spring of the year, the time when kings go out to battle … David remained in Jerusalem" (2 Samuel 11:1 NRSV). We do not know if David was battle-weary or bored, but we know he took his eyes off God and attached his gaze to a bathing Bathsheba, the wife of one of his elite fighting men, Uriah. *Read 2 Samuel 11:1–17, 26–27.*

When David lamented his friend Jonathan in 2 Samuel 1:26, he said a curious thing: "I grieve for you, Jonathan my brother; you were very dear to me. Your love for me was wonderful, more wonderful than that of women." When David took Bathsheba, he had at least seven wives, but clearly, David didn't have rich friendships or deep love relationships with these women. His friendship with Jonathan was treasured and deep; his relationships with his wives were seemingly shallow.

---

[24] *The Revell Bible Dictionary*, p. 279.
[25] Blackaby, Henry and Richard. *Experiencing God Day by Day*, p. 276.

While we will never know the reason David played "god" with so many lives when he took Bathsheba, we can speculate. David was alone and lonely. Years before, David had been alone when he was on the run from Saul, and he sought comfort in God.

- What could it have been about David's present situation that kept him from seeking fellowship with God?

_____

_____

_____

One problem was his DNA—his human condition. "Temptation is not something we may escape … what you go through is the common inheritance of the race," notes Oswald Chambers. He clarifies, "Temptation is a suggested short cut to the realization of the highest at which I aim—not towards what I understand as evil, but towards what I understand as good."[26]

David was without anyone who could connect with him mentally and emotionally, as Jonathan had, to keep him encouraged and grounded and loved unconditionally. In his longing, he understood that Bathsheba could at least temporarily make him feel whole and fulfilled.

In our "Just Say No" drug campaigns in school, students are conditioned to say "No" if a stranger offers them drugs. But when students are "mentored" into drug fellowship by older friends and peers, they don't see it as the evil it is; they understand it to be good as they are accepted and temporarily fulfilled.

- Have you ever been tempted by something you saw at the time as good only to discover its negative impact later?

_____

_____

_____

Read 2 Samuel 12:1–7.

David must have subconsciously known God would not have approved and purposefully kept God out of his consciousness. Bathsheba's baby had been born, and still, David didn't recognize how far he had fallen until Nathan brought it to his attention in a parable. David immediately recognized the evil in the story, but he was blind to his own sin until Nathan pointedly said, "You are the man." Only then did he understand the impact and the evil of his decisions and actions.

Are there parts of our lives that we keep out of our "God consciousness"? Are we sometimes blind to the impact and the evil of what we do? Do we have a Jonathan in our lives—someone who encourages us, grounds us, and loves us unconditionally? Do they have the courage and the compassion to tell us when our actions are questionable? Can we acknowledge and own our sin?

Read 2 Samuel 12:7–10.

"And if all this had been too little, I would have given you even more." God must have been

---

[26] Chambers, Oswald. *My Utmost for His Highest*, p. 192. September 17.

brokenhearted. The "man after [God's] own heart"[27] had strayed. How often do we break God's heart with our own yearnings, temptations, and discontent? According to Blackaby, "Discontent stems from the sin of ingratitude and a lack of faith that God loves you enough to provide for all that you need."[28] Was David discontented? He had so much, yet he was lonely and did not appreciate what he had. He wanted more.

How often do we feel the stirrings of loneliness and discontent as we yield to the ravages of our "wants." The world certainly doesn't help in its incessant messages of younger, thinner, prettier, newer, faster, smarter, etc. We confuse our wants and our needs. How many of us are in debt because of our needs versus being in debt as a result of our wants? David had power and prestige, and yet he gave in to his wants; whereas we often yield to our wants in order to get power and prestige.

Psalm 84:11 says, "For the Lord God is a sun and shield; the Lord bestows favor and honor; no good thing does he withhold from those whose walk is blameless."

- What is the difference between God's view of "good things" and our view of good things?

  _____

  _____

  _____

God has promised to withhold "no good thing" from us, so where's the disconnect? Our view of good things tends to have a worldly slant—amassing things, money, and power. God's good things are the things that sustain us and bring us peace and joy and thanksgiving. Our "good things" often take us away from God, while His good things draw us closer to Him. Do we settle for good or His best?

- Heart check: What are you thinking and feeling right now? Are you feeling the strain of bad choices you have made because of the stirrings of discontent and ingratitude?

  _____

  _____

  _____

> Our King David sat on a wall, Our King David had a great fall.
> All the King's horses and all the King's men
> Couldn't put King David back together again ...
> But God could!

Read slowly the psalm David wrote after Nathan came to him: *Psalm 51:1–17.*

David was pleading with God, "Against thee, thee only, have I sinned, and done that which is evil in thy sight ... Create in me a clean heart, O God, and put a new and right spirit within

---

[27] 1 Samuel 13:14.

[28] Blackaby, Henry and Richard. *Experiencing God Day by Day*, p. 121. April 26.

me. Cast me not away from thy presence, and take not thy Holy Spirit from me. Restore to me the joy of thy salvation, and uphold me with a willing spirit … A broken and contrite heart, O God, thou wilt not despise."[29]

Of course, God doesn't want our hearts to be broken. He just knows that when our hearts and our minds aren't on Him, they will be broken in time, and even more tragically, we'll be pulled away from Him. He wants us to be sensitive to anything that separates us from His good and perfect will.

We bring to our classrooms everything we are. Is teaching just a job to fuel our wants or to sustain our discontent? Or do we, in gratitude, teach to experience the joy of our calling?

> Gratitude becomes an act of defiant contemplation, expressing rebellion against the thousands of advertisements a year that tell you to want what you don't have, and not appreciate what you already have. Instead, gratitude celebrates what you do have …
> In so doing, it bonds the heart to the ultimate source of the gifts—God.[30]

How is God using this lesson to equip you? Record meaningful statements, ideas, and scriptures you may want to remember and use as He equips you for the task for which He is calling you.

_____

_____

_____

_____

_____

_____

_____

---

[29] Psalm 51:10–12, Revised Standard Version.
[30] McLaren, Brian. *Everything Must Change,* p. 213.

Day 5
DEALING WITH GRIEVANCES: STEPS TO FORGIVING

IT'S APPARENT THAT DAVID STRUGGLED; AS A PARENT, DO YOU STRUGGLE?

*A*S TEACHERS, WE HAVE AN edge when it comes to parenting, for in our profession, we find out pretty quickly what works and what doesn't work with kids. We deal with parents on a regular basis, and we see what "over" parenting looks like and lack of parenting and everything else in between. We deal with all types of scenarios when it comes to children and parents, so as we've dealt with and digested those experiences, it's helped our children to turn out perfectly, right? We've all heard about those "preacher's kids"; sometimes teacher's kids aren't far behind. Why is it so much easier to give advice than to know what to do in our own lives?

In Deuteronomy 17, God gave specific instructions regarding a king over Israel, and verse 17a reads, "He must not take many wives, or his heart will be led astray." Hmmm. David must have forgotten to read that verse. When David and his men got to Hebron and the men of Judah anointed him king, he had two wives, not counting Michal, Saul's daughter; but after seven years, when he was anointed king over all of Israel, he went to Jerusalem with four more wives. David now had six wives and six sons. We're not done. *Read 1 Chronicles 3:1–9.*

In Jerusalem, Bathsheba had four sons, and there were nine more sons by other wives, so how many sons did David have in all? Don't you just love word problems? How many daughters did he have? This tally doesn't even count all the sons and daughters by his concubines. Oh my. Can you spell d-y-s-f-u-n-c-t-i-o-n? Can you imagine all the posturing that went on in that household?

Review what Nathan told David about his family in *2 Samuel 12:9–14.*

The Lord told David through Nathan, "Out of your own household I am going to bring calamity upon you." Are you thinking how easy that's going to be with at least nineteen sons and one beautiful daughter? The prophesy began to unfold in the very next chapter. *Read 2 Samuel 13:1–22.*

From love to loathing, just like his father, Amnon's unchecked lust ruined lives, but Amnon didn't have a wise Nathan to confront him. Verse 22 tells us King David knew and was angry, but he disregarded his role as father and did nothing to hold his eldest son accountable. Tamar's brother, Absalom, gave David plenty of time to respond to his sister's shame, but after two years, he plotted Amnon's death. After he had Amnon killed, Absalom fled to his maternal grandfather who was king of Geshur, and there, he stayed for three years (2 Samuel 13:23–39).

Meanwhile, David "longed for Absalom," so Joab, the commander of David's army, concocted a parable spoken by a woman from Tekoa, in which she confronted David about his banished son. David recognized Joab's hand in the scheme and told Joab to bring Absalom back, but when they arrived in Jerusalem, David told Joab to put him under house arrest at his own house and refused to see him (2 Samuel 14:1–24).

- Even though David yearned for Absalom, why do you think he would not see him?

  _____

  _____

  _____

  _____

Perhaps it was pride or his position, or maybe David didn't have a clue what to say to Absalom after he had made such a mess of his own life, but two years passed, and Absalom probably got more frustrated and bitter each day. He wondered why David had him brought back, for at least in Geshur, he had a life. He forced the issue, and David agreed to see him, but apparently, it was too little too late, for immediately, Absalom plotted to usurp Israel from David's hand. Four years later, Absalom had quite a following, and the rebellion was set into motion.

For eleven years, Absalom's bitterness grew. He waited for David to reach out to him with the love and guidance of a father, but David had refused his role as a parent and kept trying to be the only thing he knew how to be to his children, their king. The country, he could control—his sons, he could not. After David was told, "The hearts of the men of Israel are with Absalom," he told his officials, "We must flee" (2 Samuel 14:28–15:14). Because David abdicated his role as father, he would now have to abdicate his throne.

How many children do you see each day whose parents don't parent? They may be too busy doing their jobs—maybe their work is king. Parenting is hard work after a long day of work. Like David, they may not know how to parent. Isn't it scary how many households are being run by five-year-olds? You see the repercussions of that scenario every day at school. Absalom needed his father's unconditional love, along with direction and discipline. When he didn't get it, he rebelled. Children will push their limits until someone finally sets them.

Family dynamics are so complex. Everyone comes to the table with a different perspective, and it's amazing how easily grudges grow into grievances when left unattended.

- Can you think of an incident growing up where a grudge intensified into a real problem for you or a family member?

  _____

  _____

  _____

  _____

- Did parents or an adult seek to disarm the situation?

_____

_____

_____

- Was the intervention effective?

_____

_____

_____

As temptations can birth full-fledged sin, grievances fueled by bitterness can spawn hatred that will poison the soul and destroy lives. Amnon was dead. Tamar was "a desolate woman"—the walking dead. Absalom was consumed with bitterness and was determined to punish his preoccupied father by taking away the thing that meant most to David—his kingdom.

Read 2 Samuel 18:1–15 and 31–33.

"O my son Absalom! My son, my son Absalom! If only I had died instead of you—O Absalom, my son, my son!" Way too little, way too late. If David had shown that kind of love and concern for Absalom when he was alive during the eleven years that his son was being eaten up by David's paternal apathy, how different things could have been.

What about our families? Are we fully present for our children, lovingly providing guidance and boundaries? What about our students? We can't be a substitute parent, but we can provide them expectations for their classroom family. What about your colleagues—your campus family? Are there any issues which have strained relationships on your campus?

- Are there "elephants in the room" at your school, issues that are being denied or ignored?

_____

_____

_____

Teachers make a host of decisions daily that impact students and their families, colleagues, and their own families. One harsh or unwise word from or to a tired teacher could have far-reaching repercussions and could start a grudge snowballing into crushing hurt. "The person who angers you, conquers you,"[31] and what's more, the person could be completely unaware of the perceived hurt.

What if the damage has already been done and the rub is irritated, blistered, and infected? Unforgiveness works that way—inching, eating, consuming. Ask Absalom. "By not forgiving, you are not hurting the person who hurt you ... you are only hurting yourself," explains Paul J. Meyer in his book *Forgiveness…The Ultimate Miracle*. The only way to get your freedom from bitterness and hurt is to forgive.

Meyer offers wise steps to pave the way to forgiveness and perhaps reconciliation. "It is

---

[31] Meyer, Paul J. *Forgiveness … The Ultimate Miracle*, p. 4.

impossible to get past a hurt that you cannot define," so first, honestly acknowledge the hurt and grieve or cry or be sad, but deal with the pain. Then state why you want to forgive. If unforgiveness gives the other person control, then forgiveness puts you in control. "By choosing to forgive, you are deciding what you want to do with your hurt. Instead of letting bitterness fester, you are deciding that you want to put the issue to rest."

Next, Meyer says to verbalize your forgiveness *to yourself.* "With the person you are choosing to forgive and the incident clear in your mind, declare, 'I forgive you for what you did. I release you. I declare I am free!'" You may want to invite God into your prayerful conversation as a witness. He can aid your efforts to do the next step—bury the offense. Leave it alone; don't pick it back up, don't dig it up. God can even help you show love to this person and pray for them. By doing these things, you are nurturing change in the person. Don't expect change, but don't cease to offer prayerful support.

"It takes one person to forgive, but two people to mend a relationship," offers Meyer. Show them acts of love, even a smile, pray for them, and be open to reconciliation, but whether it happens or not, move on past your hurt. Do something positive with your energy. Don't spend another minute stewing about the past; focus on the future.

Note that some hurts are so grievous and so deep that professional help may be necessary. Many school districts have employee assistance programs in place to provide free or reasonable counseling services. If you find you can't go forward with your life, prayerfully consider this option.

"O my son Absalom! My son, my son Absalom!" The wages of unforgiveness are hauntingly apparent in this parent. It was too late for Absalom. It was too late for David, but it's not too late for you.

As we close our study of David, we remember the young shepherd boy whose unrelenting trust in God slayed the giants of doubt and fear. God raised up a warrior, musician, king, and poet, who ushered in some of Israel's proudest days. But we remember David also as a fallible human like us, who taught us to pour out our hearts to God in every circumstance and to keep our eyes on Him and be mindful of His boundaries as we continually seek His will and His way.

How is God using this lesson to equip you? Record meaningful statements, ideas, and scriptures you may want to remember and use as He equips you for the task for which He is calling you.

_____

_____

_____

_____

_____

_____

GROUP QUESTIONS FOR DAVID WAS CALLED

- Do you struggle with anyone whose position exceeds his/her passion? What would the Lord have you do?

- Eliab was angry with David that he would even think about fighting Goliath. How often is fear the root of your anger? If you can deal with the fear, will that relieve your anger?

- Discuss the difference between appeasing God and pleasing God. What would that look like in your job?

- List and discuss the six steps in dealing with anguish from Psalm 142. Is that akin to expressing anger as a result of fear? Do you find Beth Moore's example of sorting the laundry helpful in dealing with your anguish/fear?

- List and discuss the six characteristics of leadership shown by David.

- Think about David's integrity—that he wouldn't kill Saul because Saul was the Lord's anointed. Now look at one of the examples of David's wisdom—he was supposed to "raid and plunder Israel," but instead, he wiped out Israel's enemies. Is there a disconnect here between integrity and wisdom? Explain.

- Discuss the question from Day 3: Have you ever considered your refusal to disrespect one who is in a leadership position over you as a way of honoring God?

- Can you do anything about one of the "elephants" residing at your school/job because of the lessons learned from the life of David? Would this mean more or fewer spears of injustice that you would have to dodge?

Esther Was Called

WEEK 3

Day 1

LACK OF LEADERSHIP IGNITES MANIPULATION AND PRIDE

XERXES'S LEADERSHIP STYLE WAS NO LEADERSHIP; HAVE YOU HAD THIS EXPERIENCE?

*D*UST OFF THE BOOK OF Esther and unstick the pages of this rarely used literary gem that's nestled between Nehemiah and Job. Soap opera writers would be hard pressed to come up with plots more dramatic and characters more colorful than those on the pages of Esther.

It sounds like a reality show network with the plot going something like this:

> Xerxes, *Joe Millionaire*, ruler of a vast empire had *No Boundaries*, and he held banquets exhibiting *Lifestyles of the Rich and Famous* and had *Dancing with the Stars*. He ordered Queen Vashti to make an appearance, but she had *Dance Fever* and refused; therefore, she became the *Biggest Loser* and a member of the *Ex-Wives Club*. *The Marriage Ref* recommended an *Extreme Makeover*, for they were experiencing the *Fear Factor* that *Real Housewives* would make them *Desperate Husbands*. There was *The Amazing Race* and a *Star Search* for the next queen. They searched *Persia's Got Talent*, *Project Runway*, *Persian Idol*, even *Jersey Shore* for *The Contender* who might become *Paris Hilton's My New BFF*. They were even *Keeping Up with the Kardashians*. Finally, *The Bachelor* showed he was *Smarter Than a 5ᵗʰ Grader* and chose Esther, *The Survivor*. Then *Big Brother*, Mordecai, who was *The Mole*, overheard *Murder in Smalltown X*, and he was rewarded by *The Apprentice*, Haman, who was later found by the *Undercover Boss*, Xerxes, to be *The Weakest Link* and was *Punk'd*. They probably all belong in *Celebrity Rehab*.[32]

If you've read the Book of Esther, you know that was a pretty accurate recap. All you overachievers may want to read the whole book of Esther—it only has ten action-packed chapters, but do *read Esther 1* now.

Did you teachers get that? A hundred eighty days of partying and then seven more days of staff development partying, probably to eat up all the leftovers. Did the teaching contract you signed call for a 187-day "banquet"?

According to Esther 1:3, "The military leaders of Persia and Media, the princes, and the nobles

---

[32] http://www.realitytvworld.com/realitytvworld/allshows.shtml.

of the provinces were present" at the banquets. It was probably a "revolving door" banquet with princes and officials from each of the 127 provinces coming on an appointed day rather than all being together for 180 days.[33] You know how hard it is to keep twenty-two students engaged for that many days, so hopefully, it wasn't the whole crew for all that time.

King Xerxes* was born with the proverbial "silver spoon" in his mouth. His grandfather, Cyrus the Great, King of Persia, conquered Babylon and opened the way for the Hebrew exiles to go back and rebuild the temple in Jerusalem (see Ezra 1:1–4). Cyrus's daughter, Atossa, married Darius I, who became King of Persia, and while Xerxes was not Darius's eldest son, he was the eldest son of Darius and Atossa, and her "special position enabled Xerxes to succeed his father."[34]

Xerxes's father, Darius, "is best known in history for his unsuccessful invasion of Europe which was stopped by the Greeks at Marathon."[35] Besides checking in with the leadership of each province, most commentaries believe the main reason for the lengthy banquet season was to reassure provincial leaders of Persia's great wealth and stability as Xerxes sought support to invade and conquer Greece. Xerxes was going to make them feel important, impress them with his "riches beyond measure" décor, and then "let" them help him make the world his empire. Do you smell manipulation here?

Enter Queen Vashti, but the problem is she doesn't enter, and it's a huge embarrassment to Xerxes before his probably very drunken attendees. Remember Esther 1:8? The guests could have as much wine as they wanted. Esther 1:10–11 says, "King Xerxes was in high spirits from wine" when he commanded his servants to fetch "Queen Vashti, wearing her royal crown, in order to display her beauty." "Some suggest this summons meant she was to wear only the royal crown."[36]

According to Matthew Henry, writing his commentary on Esther in 1708,

> If he [Xerxes] had not been put out of the possession of himself by drinking to excess, he would not have done such a thing, but would have been angry at any one that should have mentioned it. When the wine is in the wit is out, and men's reason departs from them.[37]

Well, "the wit" was definitely out as Xerxes put Queen Vashti in an untenable situation. Her choices were (a) to be loyal to the king and go before a banquet hall full of drunken men dressed in her crown and royal birthday suit or (b) to defy the king and refuse to appear.

---

*NIV uses Xerxes, other translations use Ahasuerus as King of Persia.

[33] Henry, Matthew. *Matthew Henry's Commentary: Joshua to Esther*, v. 2, p. 1,122. McLean, Virginia: MacDonald Publishing Company. ISBN 0-917006-21-6.

[34] Schmitt, Rüdiger (1989). "Atossa." *Encyclopaedia Iranica*, vol. 3. Encyclopaedia Iranica Foundation. ISBN 0710091214.

[35] *The Revell Bible Dictionary*, p. 278, Darius.

[36] Humphreys, W. Lee. "Esther, Esther with the Additions" in *HarperCollins Study Bible*, p. 738. New York, New York: HarperCollins Publishers, 1993.

[37] Henry, 1124.

- Have you ever been put into a no-win situation at school?

_____

_____

_____

- In your opinion, was pride involved? Their pride or yours?

_____

_____

_____

Xerxes, master of the realm from Ethiopia to India, was seemingly not even master of his own household; he was humiliated and enraged. Instead of obedience, Queen Vashti struck a spark in Xerxes's alcohol-soaked ego, and it blew up into a fire that burned all wives of the realm.

Since it was a very public refusal, Xerxes consulted "the sages who knew the laws" (Esther 1:13), for the consequence of her refusal would also have to be very public. There's something interesting about the Persian consultations according to Beth Moore:

> The Greek historian Herodotus wrote that the Persians would "deliberate about the gravest matters when they are drunk, and what they approve in their counsels is proposed to them the next day by the master of the house where they deliberate, when they are now sober and if being sober they still approve it, they act thereon, but if not, they cast it aside. And when they have taken counsel about a matter when sober, they decide upon it when they are drunk." As strange as the idea is to us, the ancient Persians believed they could reach further into the spiritual world when they were intoxicated.[38]

Absolutely no comment about deliberations of state legislatures, state education agencies, and local school boards!

Apparently, the "spirits," wine, made Memucan immediately think how this event would play out in his own household, that "there will be no end of contempt and wrath," for he seemed more concerned about himself and the other men than about the king. He advised that Vashti should lose her position, and *by law*, all women should "give honor to their husbands, high and low alike." (Esther 1:18-19 NRSV)

- When is the last time you remember everyone being punished for the "sins" of one?

_____

_____

_____

---

[38] Moore, Beth. *Esther*, p. 26.

- Does it ever happen in education?

_____

_____

_____

It's hard to legislate respect, isn't it? Respect is something that has to be earned, and for leaders and heads of organizations, and even households, to enact a law requiring obedience and respect boomerangs back at them as faulty leadership in their heavy-handedness.

What do we learn from Xerxes? Maybe he half-heartedly picked up the warrior baton to conquer Greece, he fostered that vision during the banquets, but in all other instances in the Book of Esther, he ceded his authority to others, and it became a royal mess. If Xerxes were a quarterback, he didn't call the plays; in fact, he didn't even touch the ball!

A leader must define his/her vision for an organization and foster that vision in others. Growing and nurturing a shared vision does not include manipulation or pridefully forcing someone into an oppressive, no-win situation. Leadership should not be a power-struggle. Unless an organization or school works together toward a common goal, accomplishment will not be maximized. Someone has to call the play, then the whole team has to execute it. The power comes when the whole team works together.

Xerxes' reluctant and absent leadership is contrasted to that of the wise and humble shepherds, Moses and David. Moses shepherded a resistant, fledgling nation, while David led a battle-weary, splintered nation into its glorious heyday. We, too, are called to shepherd—teachers shepherd their students and administrators shepherd teachers, staff, and students. Of final importance, Xerxes counciled with "the sages who knew the laws" while Moses and David kept council with God. Which one will we choose?

Tune in tomorrow for the Miss Persia pageant, same time, same channel!

How is God using this lesson to equip you? Record meaningful statements, ideas, and scriptures you may want to remember and use as He equips you for the task for which He is calling you.

_____

_____

_____

_____

_____

_____

Day 2

PRETENTIOUSNESS AND SELFISHNESS VERSUS MATURITY AND DEPTH

BEAUTY IS SKIN DEEP, BUT UGLY IS TO THE BONE.

*T*HERE WAS A CLOTHING FAD several years ago: girls wearing pink shorts with "Princess" across the seat. They may even have a "Princess" shirt to match. Did these little girls behave like princesses too?

- In general, how would you describe their behavior?

  _____

  _____

  _____

- Do these little girls get along well with their peers?

  _____

  _____

  _____

Let's enter the time machine and whisk ourselves back into the fifth century, to 480 BC, by reading *Esther 2:1–18*.

Four years have passed, and Xerxes is licking his wounds from "a disastrously unsuccessful expedition to Greece, suffered naval defeat at Salamis, and was chased like a girl out of Plataea."[39] OUCH! Xerxes is moping around the palace to be sure, so "the king's personal attendants" propose that he become "The Bachelor." King Xerxes was depressed but not dead, so he issued the edict and elaborate plans were made to bring young virgins from far and wide.

Enter Esther, meaning "star" in Persian, a.k.a. Hadassah, or "myrtle" in Hebrew; but she kept that name quiet at the directive of her cousin, Mordecai, who adopted her after she had been orphaned at some point during the Jewish exile. The diaspora began when the Babylonians conquered and carried away many of Israel's upper-class and able-bodied citizens in 597 BC, with final destruction of the temple in Jerusalem, and the last wave of exiles in 86 BC.[40] Mordecai's family, from the tribe of Benjamin, was probably part of the first wave of exiles with King Jehoiachin.[41]

---

[39] Moore, Beth. *Esther*, p. 36.
[40] *The Revell Bible Dictionary*, p. 120.
[41] *HarperCollins Study Bible*, p. 739.

In 539 BC, Cyrus, king of Persia, conquered Babylon and allowed the Jews to go back and rebuild Jerusalem. Many Jewish families stayed, apparently Mordecai and Esther's families among them, so at this point, they had been living as aliens for 110 years. This Jewish population, by and large, blended into the culture with no outward signs of their ancestral practices; however, "Prejudice against Jews was obviously already in motion in Persia,"[42] so Mordecai advised Esther not to bring up her heritage.

Can you imagine what this queen-search looked like? Each of the 127 provinces had a commissioner whose job it was to search for and bring young girls to the harem at Susa. If each one brought three or four, that's between four hundred and five hundred girls. Some girls were probably eager for the adventure, while other girls were taken from their families and stripped of their aspirations.

No matter their state of mind, they were going to get "the royal treatment." They had plenty of food to fatten them up, and Esther 2:12 tells us the girls had beauty treatments for a year—"six months with oil of myrrh and six months with perfumes and cosmetics." In addition, "When the girl went in to the king, she was given whatever she asked for to take with her from the harem to the palace" (Esther 2:12–13).

With rampant anxiety and posturing, along with constant barometric pressure changes from the PMS and "cat fights," there was probably a storm brewing all the time. Beth Moore refers to the Book of Esther as the "Book of Estrogen"; can you just imagine? It was a guy's dream and a young girl's nightmare. At the end of the regimen, do you think they wore pink shorts under their tunics that had "Princess" across the seat?

- Try to envision these chosen ones. How would you describe their behavior?

  _____

  _____

  _____

- Do you think these girls got along well with their peers?

  _____

  _____

  _____

Compare these answers with your answers at the beginning.
Read Esther 2:8–9.

- What do you think it was about Esther that so quickly pleased Hegai that he would give her preferential treatment?

  _____

  _____

  _____

---

[42] Moore, Beth. *Esther*, p. 44.

Oswald Chambers says, "Sorrow burns up a great amount of shallowness, but it does not always make a man better. Suffering either gives me my self or it destroys my self."[43] In her young life, Esther had been through the fires of sorrow. She and her family lived as exiles in a prejudicial, alien environment, and she had lost not just one parent but both her parents. As an orphan, she would be swallowed up in grief and bitterness and despair, or she would be refined through the fire of sorrow.

- Have you "found" yourself in sorrow? What was it, and how did it change you?

_____

_____

_____

_____

Esther found herself. A great difference between Esther and the other princesses was the absence of shallowness in her. "Esther won the favor of everyone who saw her" (Esther 2:15b). That's an incredible statement in a harem with several hundred other girls.

Chambers continues, "You always know the man who has been through the fires of sorrow and received himself, you are certain you can go to him in trouble and find that he has ample leisure for you … If you receive yourself in the fires of sorrow, God will make you nourishment for other people."[44]

Esther was not conceited, she was real, *Velveteen Rabbit* real. She may not have looked it on the outside, but inside, she had some big scars and more than a few ripped seams. The miraculous thing was that it didn't embitter her but made her more loving. She listened to and respected other people; she didn't try to manipulate them or take them for granted. She knew who she was; therefore, she could nurture others and make others comfortable around her.

Sorrow melts away pretentiousness and selfishness. It provides a compass of what is important and what is not. Trivial things are folly to one who is grounded in this way. It's no wonder our bachelor fell in love with her and crowned this young orphaned Jewish girl his queen.

Does this mean one can't become real without experiencing sorrow? No, life experience has a way of sifting us until all that's left is the real us, but in one as young as Esther, sorrow quickened the process. There aren't many shortcuts to maturity.

- How does one learn to recognize pretentiousness and selfishness in ourselves?

_____

_____

_____

_____

---

[43] Chambers, Oswald. *My Utmost for His Highest*, p. 128.
[44] Chambers, Oswald. *My Utmost for His Highest*, p. 129.

- How can we become more real with others?

  _____

  _____

  _____

- How do we deal with colleagues who lack maturity? How would Esther deal with them?

  _____

  _____

  _____

- How can we teach the "princes" and "princesses" in our classes the need to walk past their selfishness/shallowness and become more loving and more mature in their relationships with others?

  _____

  _____

  _____

Esther's sorrow was turned to joy as Xerxes "placed the glass slipper on her foot." As the _Young and the Restless_ and _The Bold and the Beautiful_ watched her walk down the aisle under the _Guiding Light_, they knew they had _One Life to Live_, and they were _Searching for Tomorrow_ and wondering how to live _The Days of Our Lives_.

Did Queen Esther and Xerxes live "happily ever after"? Stay tuned.

How is God using this lesson to equip you? Record meaningful statements, ideas, and scriptures you may want to remember and use as He equips you for the task for which He is calling you.

_____

_____

_____

_____

_____

_____

Day 3

HAVE YOU EVER HAD YOUR JOY STOLEN?

FAMILY FEUD ON STEROIDS

$\mathcal{H}$ERE'S YOUR QUESTION ON *Family Feud*: Name a biblical family rivalry that started in the womb. Slap, DING! "Jacob and Esau." You're right!

Here's the scoop: When Abraham was seventy-five years old, God appeared to him, made a covenant with him, and told him he would be the father of many nations. Twenty-five years later, a long-awaited son, Isaac, was born to Sarah and Abraham. Isaac married Rebekah, who had a very difficult pregnancy with twins. The babies were fighting each other in her womb; she said to the Lord, "I can't endure this ... And he told her, 'The sons in your womb shall become two rival nations. One will be stronger than the other, and the older shall be a servant of the younger!'"[45]

Esau appeared first with the second baby boy, Jacob, clutching Esau's heel. Later Esau sold his birthright to Jacob for a bowl of stew, and two chapters later, Jacob deceived Isaac to get the blessing meant for Esau. How's that for brotherly love? Jacob ran for his life.

Esau had a son, Eliphaz, who had a son, Amalek (1900 BC), who is the ancestral source of the Amalekites. Agag, a title given to Amalekite kings,[46] and the Amalekites were natural predators of the Israelites, attacking the weak and lagging Israelites during their Exodus march through the wilderness.

Jacob had a son, Benjamin, who, after a whole bunch of begats, was the ancestor of Kish, who had a son, Saul, the first King of Israel (1050 BC). King Saul was given the order by God through the prophet Samuel to destroy the Amalekites, largely as revenge for their deadly raids on the Exodus Israelites. Saul *almost* followed his orders, but he saved King Agag and the best livestock (1 Samuel 15). Because of his disobedience, God rejected Saul as king, and Samuel killed Agag.

Please *read Esther 2:19–3:15.*

Sooooooooooo *Who Wants to Be a Millionaire?* Here's your question: If Saul and Samuel wiped out the Amalekites (circa 1012 BC), how could Haman, the Agagite, have been a descendant of the Amalekites?

A.   The Bible is wrong.

B.   One Amalekite was disguised as a cow.

C.   Saul missed a few.

D.   A few were flying kites.

---

45   Genesis 25:22–23, Living Bible, p. 63.
46   *The Revell Bible Dictionary*, p. 1,052.

Do you need a lifeline? Answer: C. "*1 Chronicles 4:42–43* says that in the days of King Hezekiah, about 300 years later, 500 men from the tribe of Simeon killed the rest of the Amalekites, who had apparently escaped before Saul could get to them. This helps explain why God was so angry with Saul, and also how Haman could have been a descendant of King Agag."[47]

Final *Jeopardy* question: Who were the two antagonists in the Book of Esther whose rivalry goes all the way back to Rebekah's womb?

Your final *Jeopardy* answer: Who were Haman and Mordecai?

All right, *Let's Make a Deal*—no more game shows.

We are not told why Xerxes "promoted" Haman, the Agagite/Amalekite, to second in command of his empire or why the king commanded everyone to bow to Haman. "Ironically Haman is rewarded for no stated reason, while Mordecai is not rewarded in 2:19–23 for service to the king."[48] After reading about the plot Haman cooked up to get rid of Mordecai, it's not hard to imagine the behind-the-scenes conniving that took place to make his meteoric advancement happen. The power-shift that occurs in only a few verses serves to stoke the inherent rivalry between the two men.

There are so many ironies at play here. Mordecai sat at the king's gate, so it is likely that he was a government employee providing security for the king. For Haman, Mordecai provided anything but security. In fact, Mordecai's presence and his refusal to show obeisance to him made him very insecure. According to Beth Moore, "Insecurity is at the heart of every rivalry."[49]

- Explain the above quote. Do you think it's true?

  _____

  _____

  _____

- Give an example of this in the school environment.

  _____

  _____

  _____

Haman would have been angry with anyone who didn't bow, for he was a prideful man, but when he found out Mordecai was a Jew, centuries of ancestral rage boiled within him, and the situation escalated into "destroy, kill, and annihilate." For a second time within three chapters, the "sins" of one person penalize many.

For us, this story is extreme, but on a daily basis, we may participate in various degrees of rivalry. It could exhibit itself as defensiveness with a situation or person with whom we've had a negative experience. Prejudice, while very subtle, could manifest itself as mocking, satirizing, or ridiculing someone "in the name of fun" or perhaps feigning concern for them. People's prejudices

---

[47] http://gracethrufaith.com/ask-a-bible-teacher/was-haman-really-an-agagite/.

[48] Humphreys, W. Lee. *HarperCollins Study Bible*, p. 741.

[49] Moore, Beth. *Esther*. Session 2 video lecture, 2008.

are aired by the jokes they tell, the e-mails they send, their leisure time activities, and the company they keep. Prejudice becomes even more pronounced when we talk to others about a person or situation and begin drawing them in, thus creating a power base. Does any of this sound familiar?

- List some of the places in the school environment that may be hazardous to our spiritual health as far as prejudice is concerned:

  _____

  _____

  _____

How about the "busybodies" who went to Mordecai first and then to Haman and poured gasoline on his pride? People like them stir up trouble and then stand back and watch the explosion with an "oh so innocent" look on their faces. Do you have any of those on your campus?

Haman's lies easily convinced the uninterested Xerxes to issue a decree for the "destruction" of the Jews, "to destroy, to kill, and to annihilate all Jews, young and old, women and children." It's reminiscent of Samuel's declaration to Saul for the destruction of the Amalekites in 1 Samuel 15:1–3. As the last courier gallops off, Xerxes and Haman sit down for happy hour, completely unaffected by the mass death sentence they just issued.

The next time we see Haman in Esther 5:9, he is still "on top of the world" in excited anticipation of wiping the disrespect right off Mordecai's face. *Read* the rest of *5:9–14* to see what happened next.

Mordecai was pretty quick, wasn't he? He stole Haman's joy in broad daylight without a single witness. That's what happens when our happiness is on the surface in outward trappings and not tucked away in our hearts. Haman went home and counted his blessings, but he said, "Yet all this does me no good so long as I see the Jew Mordecai sitting at the king's gate," seemingly impervious to the havoc Haman has laid at his feet. Haman wanted power over Mordecai, yet Mordecai still had power over Haman. Haman had a chink in his prideful armor, and all his joy has leaked right out.

- Have you let someone steal your joy lately? Who took it?

  _____

  _____

  _____

Was your joy stolen when the edgy parent note pricked and deflated your wonderful day? *The nerve of her to criticize me over* _____ *when she is always* _____. Did it get away from you when your administrator pointedly looked at his watch as you hurried to pick up your kids from an activity? *He's the hall police … He must have a pretty easy job since that's all he does … He's always trying to catch me.* Remember: Defensiveness is the first step in rivalry. If you sit around and fret and grumble about it, will you be tempted to ridicule or mock as you tell someone else about it so they can commiserate with you? That's the scaffolding of a rivalry.

Disassemble it right now. If you were wrong, admit it to yourself, and ask God to forgive you, and soften your embarrassed heart toward your Mordecai. If you were *not* wrong in the situation, then pray for that other person because their attack was not about you at all—it was about what's going on in their own lives. You just happened to be their "last straw." Don't take ownership of that one; duck and let their venom hit somewhere else.

When you interact with so many personalities during a day as you do at school, it's very easy to become a catcher's mitt for negativity, barbs, and anxiety in general. Field and deal with only the things that are true, and the rest, let it go. Don't let anyone steal the joy that you know in your heart. Rest in the One who parted the sea and shepherded His chosen to the Promised Land. Rest in the One who raised a lowly Jewish orphan girl to be queen over an empire.

OK, one more game—*The Price is Right*. How much is this worth—the joy of knowing we are held in the loving hands of One who can do all things? Yes, that's right—it's *priceless*.

How is God using this lesson to equip you? Record meaningful statements, ideas, and scriptures you may want to remember and use as He equips you for the task for which He is calling you.

Day 4

CHOOSING LIFE IN THE MIDST OF CATASTROPHE

ESTHER'S "DEFINING MOMENT"; WHAT DEFINES YOU?

*W*E LEFT ESTHER AS SHE was "walking down the aisle" toward Xerxes who crowned her queen of Persia. Now fast forward five years: Esther had finally gotten used to the idea of being queen and has been enjoying the perks of that exalted station, when her servants rushed in to tell her something was wrong with Mordecai. "He has put on sackcloth and ashes and is wailing in the streets!" they reported. What a shock for Esther! She immediately sent Hathach, one of the king's eunuchs, to find out what was wrong.

Read Esther 4.

Mordecai had just heard of the king's edict, and he had stepped out of his guise as a Persian official and into his Jewish heritage. When most Jews would be tempted to bury themselves deeper into the Persian culture, Mordecai very humbly and very publicly stood up to take his place with his Jewish brothers. Traditionally, "Sackcloth and ashes symbolized not only the Jews' poverty of spirit before the Lord but their complete deadness without Him."[50] We don't know Mordecai's spiritual mindset, but according to the edict, he was already dead, so his only hope was the God of his fathers and Esther.

Part of the shock Esther experienced was Mordecai's change in game plan. For years, he had told her not to bring up her Jewish background, and all of a sudden, he openly embraced it. Hathach told her all that had happened and even handed her a copy of the edict so she could read it herself, but don't you imagine he rather haltingly told her of Mordecai's charge to her? Hathach knew it was a death sentence for her to approach the king uninvited. Esther was aghast, not only that her beloved cousin would ask her to take a risk such as this, but also that the order had come from her husband, a weak leader, but not an evil man.

At his second meeting with Hathach, Mordecai gave probably the most famous speech of all the Esther scripture. In Mordecai's message to Esther, he said, "Do not think that because you are in the king's house you alone of all the Jews will escape. For if you remain silent at this time, relief and deliverance for the Jews will arise from another place, but you and your father's family will perish. And who knows but that you have come to royal position for such a time as this?" (Esther 4:13–14)

Do you think Esther felt the same adrenalin flush you did when you were diagnosed with

---

[50] Moore, Beth. *Esther*, p. 86.

cancer? Or when you found out your loved one had been killed in a car wreck? Or when your loved one told you s/he wanted a divorce? Or when the tornado erased your house and everything you owned? Or when … Or when … Or when. The aftermath is the same: Your life has changed, and you'll either die in your old life or you'll have to choose to live.

- Have you ever experienced an earth-shaking loss? Briefly describe it.

  _____

  _____

  _____

- Do you remember thinking, "I can't do this?"

  _____

  _____

  _____

We can faint, we can "pitch a fit," we can cry until we're exhausted, but things will never be the same. We can look up at the sky during the night and wonder how the stars can still shine; how can the world still revolve around the sun when our life has been knocked off its axis? We fall asleep exhausted and wake up from the same bad dream. The only thing that is unchanged is the fact that we have to change. We have to choose life.

- Do you remember at what point you "chose life"?

  _____

  _____

  _____

Read one of the last entreaties Moses made to the Israelites before they crossed the Jordan to go into the Promised Land in Deuteronomy 30:19–20:

> [19]This day I call heaven and earth as witnesses against you that I have set before you life and death, blessings and curses. Now choose life, so that you and your children may live [20]and that you may love the Lord your God, listen to his voice, and hold fast to him. For the Lord is your life, and he will give you many years in the land he swore to give to your fathers, Abraham, Isaac and Jacob.

- What are the four reasons why you should "choose life"?

  1)

  2)

  3)

  4)

- "For the Lord is your life." What does that mean to you on a personal level?

_____

_____

_____

Courage. It took courage—raw, ugly, lock-jawed courage—when the very last thing she felt was courageous. That's how Esther felt when she agreed to approach the king, adding, "If I perish, I perish." According to Redmon, "Courage is not the absence of fear, but the judgment that something more important is at stake."[51] Not only her life but also the lives of all the Jews depended on her; but she knew she could not do it in her own power.

- What did she request of Mordecai?

_____

_____

_____

For Lori, her edict was given by her principal. As the only physical education teacher at a large elementary school, she had been concerned about deep cuts her school district was going to have to make because of the massive shortfall of state money, but her program had been exemplary according to parents and administration. After all, she had been teacher of the year at her school. She told herself not to worry.

Her principal told her he had fought for her, but there were too many coaches in the district, so they were being shifted down. Now a high school PE teacher was being assigned to her position. Flatly, the quality of her program didn't matter, nor did the fact that often she willingly went "above and beyond" her duties writing grants and taking on responsibilities that were of benefit to the school at large. She was out of a job, but because she had an elementary classroom certification, she was offered a job as a fourth-grade teacher, though she hadn't been in a classroom in twenty-six years.

Catastrophic? Yes, her whole career had been turned upside down. As her mind was whirling between "It's not fair" and "At least I have a job," she called on her friends to pray—pray that God would be glorified in all this, pray for direction, pray that God's perfect will be done, pray to uphold her up as she did the last thing she wanted to do—return to school the very next day. Lori and Queen Esther both knew they couldn't do it in their own power, and they called for prayer. The network of prayer gave them the strength to step out in faith, to step into a moment that defined both of them.

Esther was called to deliver the Jews just as Moses was called to deliver them. They faced two of the most powerful men on earth who held their lives in their hands—or did they? Xerxes and the pharaoh probably thought they were in control, but it was God who led and strengthened

---

[51] Redmon. From Beth Moore video session 4 of *Esther*.

Esther and Moses. "The saint is hilarious when he is crushed with difficulties because the thing is so ludicrously impossible to anyone but God,"[52] discloses Oswald Chambers.

As for Lori, she begins her new school year next week, and she is stepping out in faith, absolutely trusting God. Those of us who know her have seen her being refined as gold in the crucible over the last several months, as she has faced giving up her passion. Her steadfast faith has spoken volumes about trusting God and being about His agenda and not her own.

And who knows, Lori, but that you have come to this position for such a time as this? You are queen of our hearts!

> Doing God's will and thus experiencing suffering is still the highest
> form of faith, and the most glorious Christian achievement.[53]

How is God using this lesson to equip you? Record meaningful statements, ideas, and scriptures you may want to remember and use as He equips you for the task for which He is calling you.

_____

_____

_____

_____

_____

_____

_____

---

[52] Chambers, Oswald. *My Utmost for His Highest*, p. 157.
[53] Parkhurst, Charles. *Streams in the Desert*, p. 278.

Day 5

COINCIDENCE OR PRESENCE?

ROYAL COMEUPPANCE; ROYAL RESIDENT

AFTER THE THREE DAYS OF fasting and prayer, there's no sackcloth and ashes for Esther, no young Jewish girl groveling before the king. She dressed in royal robes with the crown perched on her well-coiffed head to come before Xerxes as Esther, Queen of Persia, fully believing she is queen for this very encounter.

The custom in Persia was that anyone who appeared before the king would die. "Only a person summoned by the king could visit him without penalty. This gave dignity to the monarch and protected him from assassination."[54]

Imagine the shock that gripped the king's hall as the Queen of Persia stepped into view. Never looking more regal or more beautiful, Esther took everyone's breath away as they awaited King Xerxes's reaction. Thankfully, his scepter reached out to her as he voiced his approval of her request before it was even made.

Right then and there, most of us would probably have gushed out the whole sordid plot, forcing Xerxes to choose between his trusted right-hand man and a woman he doesn't even see on a daily basis. He may even take time to remember how his last queen embarrassed him and in recalled anger, deny Esther's request, thus sentencing her to die with the rest of the Jews. This would serve to prove Haman right—those disrespectful, law-breaking Jews!

Queen Esther had a different plan. As a beloved school counselor used to say, "You attract more flies with honey than with vinegar." In Esther's case, it was wine and food—"the way to a man's heart." (Esther forgot to tell us she had already prepared a feast for three.)

Xerxes quickly rounded up Haman, and off they went to feast. During the wine at the end of the meal, Xerxes again asked Esther her request and reaffirmed that it would be granted whatever it was. ESTHER, NOW! Nope, she requested that he and Haman come again the next day for yet another banquet.

Over the next twenty-four hours, do you think Xerxes wondered why Esther was so keen on having Haman attend the banquets? "According to Dr. Levenson, Esther 'thus predisposed' the king to distrust and dislike Haman so that he'd 'grant her request to do [Haman] and his hate-filled cohorts in.' The second banquet 24 hours later would provide just enough time for Xerxes to become suspicious and angry but not enough time for him to talk himself out of it."[55]

---

[54] *Illustrated Manners and Customs*, p. 157.

[55] Moore, Beth. *Esther*, p. 114.

Is the suspense killing you? Please *read Esther 6 and 7.* You won't be disappointed.

The king had trouble sleeping and asked for a bedtime story. Coincidentally, the reader picked out a five-year-old story of Mordecai foiling a plot to kill King Xerxes. Coincidentally, it dawned on Xerxes to reward Mordecai after all these years. Coincidentally, Haman appeared just then. Coincidentally, Haman thought the king was thinking of rewarding him. Coincidentally, Haman, go do all these wonderful things you've cooked up for Mordecai, your archenemy. Is that not rich?

Haman's head was still spinning when he was whisked away to Esther's banquet along with the king. He was probably just starting to relax as he reached for the goblet of wine to drown this horrible day. Maybe he was even anticipating in amusement the queen's request; "Perhaps a regal shopping spree," he chuckled to himself as he took a big gulp of wine.

From somewhere in his daze, he heard Esther say, "I and my people … destroyed … killed … annihilated … a foe and enemy, this wicked Haman!" Can't you just see Haman spew out his mouthful of wine as Esther called out his name?

The astonished Haman saw the king angrily run outside, and he looked at Queen Esther who "coincidentally" had lost her demure demeanor. In its place was probably a "gotcha" look that has echoed down through Jewish history and probably still causes unrest in the Middle East today. Just kidding.

Haman went from having everything to having nothing. Esther and Mordecai went from death to life. King Xerxes traded one "right-hand man" for another.

"Coincidence" is a huge player in this drama. Have you figured out who this unnamed character is? Nowhere in the Book of Esther is this main character named, but His work is very evident. Yes, God is the main actor. More accurately, these "coincidences" were "God-incidences."

- When is the last time you experienced a "God-incidence"? What was it?

  _____

  _____

  _____

  _____

  _____

  _____

- How would you explain this "God-incidence" to a non-believer?

  _____

  _____

  _____

  _____

  _____

- List some of the "God-incidences" in the Book of Esther, some of the ways God provided for them:

1)

2)

3)

4)

"God-incidences" to the unbeliever are coincidences, but to the believer, they are undeniably God's hand in the drama of our lives. Was it mere chance that this Jewish orphan girl became queen of an empire? Jews had been scattered throughout the realm assimilated into the Persian culture for over one hundred years. Why now? Was God using Esther to draw those of Jewish ancestry back to their roots? Was He trying to show this generation of nonpracticing Jews His love for them and His protection and deliverance of them even as scattered as they were? Did God want them to join together in a common cause and revitalize their faith?

As with many of the important events in Jewish history, Esther's story is commemorated by an annual celebration called Purim—"Pur," casting of lots as Haman did in determining the day the edict would take place. It is a joyful occasion celebrating God's providence in turning things around for the sentenced Jews. (For more on Purim, read Esther 9:20–32.)

In the story of Esther, God delivered a people who didn't know they needed Him. He drew them back to Him. Is God drawing you back to Him? What about your story? Is God a major player in your life? Do you count on Him to provide for you when all odds are against you? Do you see "coincidences" in your life as God's messages of love and care?

Just as God's name was not used in the Book of Esther, His name is not used in the public school, but that doesn't mean He is not there. In fact, you can take Him to work with you every morning. He may even hum a praise song in your ear all day.

He could be with you at morning duty, greeting the children, and with you as your children excitedly put up their backpacks. He sees the sleepy little fellow with the empty stomach and might remind you to scoot him off to the cafeteria.

He's with you when the lesson is going well; he senses your frustration and may remind you to breathe when they just don't get it. He may not like gossiping in the teacher's lounge, but He loves going with you to playground duty and watching His children enjoy playing outside in His creation.

He can help you sense a parent's stress and deal with it lovingly. He's probably not fond of staff meetings either, but He knows they are necessary and might even remind you to bring chocolate. He loves watching you teach the children how to love and respect one another. He loves how you've figured out the children and attend to each of their needs just as He knows all about you and provides for your needs as well.

Do you remember how Haman's joy was so easily stolen because his joy was only "skin deep" in outward trappings? God loves that our joy is tucked deep in our hearts. In fact, that's how He gets to school and gets back home with us. He is our joy, and He takes royal residence. As long as He's in your heart, God will be in public school.

How is God using this lesson to equip you? Record meaningful statements, ideas, and scriptures you may want to remember and use as He equips you for the task for which He is calling you.

_____

_____

_____

_____

_____

_____

GROUP QUESTIONS FOR "ESTHER WAS CALLED"

- Would you say your school leaders try to "legislate respect" through manipulation and power struggles, or are they quarterbacking a team?

- If you are teaching at "Estrogen Elementary," what are some things Esther would tell you to help you deal with others there?

- Explain how insecurity, defensiveness, and prejudice are the scaffolding of a rivalry.

- What are some things you can do to keep others from stealing your joy?

- Oswald Chambers says, "An average view of the Christian life is that it means deliverance from trouble. It is deliverance *in* trouble, which is very different … God does not give us overcoming life: He gives us life as we overcome. The strain is the strength." How does this speak to what Esther and Lori went through?

- When in the midst of a crisis you choose life, do you have prayer warriors who will lift you up before the throne of God as did Esther and Lori? Could your study group be prayer warriors for each other?

- Share some "God-incidences" from Esther Day 5.

- Esther Day 5 portrays heightened awareness of God's presence at school. Have you had any of those experiences? How would you go about opening up the way for this dialogue to happen?

Jesus Was Called

WEEK 4

Day 1
WHERE DO YOU HANG YOUR FAITH?

TRUTH OR DARE? DO YOU DARE NOT BELIEVE THIS TRUTH?

*M*ANY WORLD RELIGIONS HOLD BELIEF in a supreme being; however, the life and teachings of Jesus are the major sticking points that separate Christianity from all other religions. While two of the major religions, Judaism and Islam, believe Jesus was a prophet, the crux of Christianity is belief in Jesus as God's Son and our Savior.

If you are participating in this Bible study, you are searching for a way to interpret truth for a richer, more meaningful life. In Jesus Christ you meet your answer head-on, for Jesus said, "I am the way and the truth and the life. No one comes to the Father except through me" (John 14:6). If you believe that passage, if you believe Jesus is who He says He is, then we must explore His way and His life.

We know of Jesus's birth from the accounts in Matthew and Luke. Matthew[56] sought to "legitimate" Jesus through a legalist Jewish male's perspective. After a lengthy genealogy linking Abraham, the father of their faith, to Jesus, "an angel of the Lord" told Joseph in a dream not to divorce Mary, his betrothed, who was with child via the Holy Spirit. The angel made it clear to him this was the child of which the prophet Isaiah spoke and that Joseph, of the lineage of David, should parent Him, along with Mary, his wife to be.[57] After the magi came to worship Jesus in Bethlehem,[58] an angel again appeared in a dream to direct Joseph to take his family to Egypt to escape murderous Herod. A third dream led Joseph to leave Egypt, again fulfilling prophecy,[59] and bring his family to Nazareth, where Jesus grew up. Matthew took pains to prove the authenticity of Jesus as Messiah to the Jews through their history and prophets.

While Luke's account also notes prophetic links to the origin of Jesus, it is much less about Jewish validation of Jesus and more about explaining the story of Jesus to a population who was not as historically bias, the Gentiles or non-Jews. Luke weaves together the story of John the Baptist and Jesus.

Recall Abraham and Sarah and the miracle birth of Isaac in the Genesis story.[60] God made a covenant with Abraham, and despite the fact that he was nearing one hundred years old and that

---

[56] Matthew 1:18–2:23.
[57] Isaiah 7:14.
[58] Micah 5:2.
[59] Hosea 11:1.
[60] Genesis 17 and 18.

Sarah, at ninety, was barren, God promised him he would be the "father of nations." Abraham believed God and, indeed, became the father of the Jewish faith.

Luke began his account with the story of Zechariah,[61] an elderly priest, to whom an angel of the Lord promised a son despite the fact that his wife, Elizabeth, was also barren. Further, the angel prophesied that the baby's name would be John, and he would be filled with the Holy Spirit, even in the womb, for he would prepare the hearts of Israel for the coming Messiah. Through John, God was preparing the sons of men for the Son of Man.

In the Old Testament, Abraham was the first man with whom God was in covenant. Zechariah, also an old man, ushered in the new covenant, a new testament, if you will, that was led by his son John. This movement would touch not only the Jewish nation, but also all nations.

The miracle conception of John did not go unnoticed, for six months later,[62] an angel of the Lord, Gabriel, appeared to Mary, a virgin but pledged to be married. In Luke 1:30, he told her, "Do not be afraid, Mary, you have found favor with God. You will be with child and give birth to a son, and you are to give him the name Jesus. He will be great and will be called the Son of the Most High." He immediately told her about her relative Elizabeth, "For nothing is impossible with God."[63]

Read the account of Mary's visit to Elizabeth in *Luke 1:39–56*, making careful note of Mary's song in verses 46–55.

Imagine how affirming it was to Mary that Elizabeth knew she was carrying the Messiah. On her journey, Mary had time to wonder and worry about her predicament and about how she would be received. Elizabeth's welcome and words must have comforted her, especially in the face of the inevitable gossip that would follow her as an unwed mother.

- What is your reaction to Mary's song?

_____

_____

_____

In verses 51–53, William Barclay points out "three revolutions which true Christianity is bound to carry out"[64]:

1. "There is a *moral* revolution. The proud are brought down. Christianity must begin by working a revolution within a man's own heart." Undoubtedly among the proud in Mary's prophetic song were the self-righteous group of Jews called Pharisees. Ironically, they who went to excruciating lengths to keep the law were deemed as the most moral of men, but Jesus' teachings often criticized their pride and underscored their lack of true morality.

---

[61] Luke 1:5–25.

[62] Luke 1:26–38.

[63] Luke 1:37.

[64] Barclay, William. *And Jesus Said: A Handbook on the Parables of Jesus*, pp. 62 and 63. Philadelphia, Pennsylvania: The Westminster Press, 1970.

"Further, when a man realizes the love of God in Christ and the lengths to which that love went, he can't but be amazed that this was done for him."

2. "There is social revolution. The mighty are brought low and those of low degree are exalted." In our society wealth, power, fame, even infamy are highly esteemed, while often common, unobtrusive, giving, and God-fearing men are disregarded. "The result is that the man whom the world accounts great may well be worthless in the kingdom of God; while the man who appears of no standing in the world may well be greatest."

3. "There is an economic revolution. The hungry are filled with good things and the rich are sent empty away. In the truly Christian state there would be such a feeling of responsibility that no one could bear to have too much while others had too little."

Further, in reference to economic revolution, Barclay quotes the American theologian B. Harvie Branscomb's[65] interpretation of this: "Business would be run not for its owners only but to support the needs of the community; no farmer would plough solely for financial gain but to feed a hungry world; no doctor or lawyer would practice for himself alone but to heal and help those in distress. Every work would be directed to the healing, the helping and the supplying of the spiritual and the physical needs of men. This would lend every task its glory; he would be greatest who was the greatest servant of all." In light of America's economic struggles of today, many would scream "socialism."

- What are your thoughts on these "revolutions"? Is this an instance of the Bible being out of touch with the times? Or are our times out of touch with the intent of the Gospels?

_____

_____

_____

Luke substantiated these revolutionary, upside-down views in his reporting of the first people to whom the announcement of Jesus's birth was made—the glory of the Lord shone around the lowly shepherds as an angel of the Lord announced, "Good tidings of great joy." Also, the shepherds were among the first visitors to the Christ child, who was born not in a palatial suite but in a stable.

While Matthew and Luke make a case for Jesus as the Son of Man, the Gospel of John clearly and elegantly expounds on Jesus, the Son of God. *Read John 1:1–18* and *Genesis 1:1–5*.

- What are your thoughts after reading these verses?

_____

_____

_____

---

[65] Branscomb, B. Harvie. Moffatt Commentary on Mark.

"In the beginning was the Word, and the Word was with God, and the Word was God. He was with God in the beginning" (John 1:1–2). "Then God said, 'Let there be … '" (Genesis 1:3) God spoke the world into existence. God's word was and is Jesus: "The Word became flesh and lived for a while among us. We have seen his glory, the glory of the one and only Son, who came from the Father, full of grace and truth." Leander E. Keck[66] says John's prologue "makes the enfleshment of the *Logos*—the Word becoming flesh—the lens through which readers are to read the story that follows. The writer of John's Gospel says, in effect, unless you read this story as the account of the Word enfleshed, you will not understand anything that matters." While Matthew and Luke tell Jesus's story beginning with His human birth and proceed to report His miracles and record His word of God's truth, the reader is convinced along the way that He is God's Son; however, John cuts to the chase and immediately espoused the divinity of Jesus.

The fourth Gospel, Mark, began with Jesus as He embarked on His ministry, but no matter which Gospel you read, the stage is quickly set for a revolution of heart and mind that literally turned contemporary thinking on its ear. It still does.

"'But what about you?' [Jesus] asked. 'Who do you say I am?'" (Luke 9:20) Just as Jesus asked this of His disciples, He is asking you as well. On this question hangs your truth.

How is God using this lesson to equip you? Record meaningful statements, ideas, and scriptures you may want to remember and use as He equips you for the task for which He is calling you.

_____

_____

_____

_____

_____

_____

_____

---

[66] Keck, Leander. *Jesus in the Gospels*, p. 217.

Day 2
JESUS RETEACHES THE LAW

FROM PRECOCIOUS YOUNG BOY TO MASTER TEACHER

*A*s MOST GIFTED CHILDREN, JESUS was totally focused on His interests, His calling. In the one Bible story of Jesus as a boy, He was drawn to the teachers in the temple while He and His family were in Jerusalem for Passover (Luke 2:41–52). He was so absorbed listening to them and asking questions that he completely missed the trip home. After a day's journey, Mary and Joseph realized Jesus wasn't among relatives and friends and backtracked to Jerusalem.

Can you imagine the scene they came upon in the temple? As Son of God, twelve-year-old Jesus pure-heartedly knew the intent of the law. Do you think the Pharisees squirmed a bit at His questioning? Even as young as He was, do you think He opened their traditional eyes to new possibilities, new interpretations? Do you think young Jesus respectfully threatened their wisdom? The proud may have been incensed at His insolence, for He was a child, but do you suppose any of them had an inkling of an idea that the young Messiah was in their midst? The uneasiness felt by the teachers and Jesus's parents was a foretaste of the awe and discomfort they would feel almost twenty years later as Jesus fully came into His ministry.

What about you? Do you foster the curiosity and creativity of precocious children, or in your push for staying on schedule, are you dismissive and short? Could you pull them aside later and have a discussion that validates their questions or concerns?

What about Jesus? Did their answers accommodate His divine knowledge? Or did their gritty responses rub and irritate the Son of God so that divine thinking, through the years, layered over them, producing the pearls of wisdom that so amazed his followers? Do you think that event began coloring Jesus's thinking about the Pharisees? As His knowledge of Hebrew law increased along with closeness to His Father, the hypocrisy of the Pharisees must have weighed heavily on Him.

According to William Barclay, "Pharisee literally means 'the separated one.' The Jewish scribes and Rabbis, beginning from the great principles of the Ten Commandments, had amplified the Jewish law until it included tens of thousands of petty regulations covering every moment and every action in life; and they considered that the keeping of these regulations was a matter of life and death … No ordinary mortal could continue within the everyday business of life and observe all these regulations."[67] Further, they considered themselves defiled to associate in any way with those who did not stringently keep the myriad of laws. The problem was not God's laws,

---

[67] Barclay, William. *And Jesus Said: A Handbook on the Parables of Jesus*, pp. 99–100. Philadelphia, Pennsylvania: The Westminster Press, 1970.

however, the problem was that the laws of man had obliterated the heart and intention of God's laws. If sin was not keeping all the Jewish laws, then ordinary Jews must have felt enchained to sin and hopelessness.

As Jesus sat on a mountainside in Matthew 5 and taught the crowds who came to Him, the stage was set for a sermon that may have resonated from the heart of a twelve-year-old Jesus. *Read Matthew 5:17–20.*

"For I tell you that unless your righteousness surpasses that of the Pharisees and the teachers of the law, you will certainly not enter the kingdom of heaven" (Matthew 5:20). Curious Pharisees in attendance probably gasped and mentally branded Jesus a heretic right then and there.

- Jesus said, "Do not think that I have come to abolish the Law or the Prophets; I have not come to abolish them but to _____" (Matthew 5:17).
- The Pharisees were all about the law, and they went to extremes to keep it and to appear pious. What do you think Jesus meant when He told the crowd they must be more righteous than the Pharisees?

_____

_____

_____

Henry and Richard Blackaby offer a test: "How do you know if you are a 'Pharisee'? When you do not have a teachable spirit. When you do not seek to hear from God, believing you already know what He thinks. When you feel that you are capable of helping others in their spiritual lives, but no one can teach you anything. Don't allow the limited knowledge you now have to blind you to the great truths God still wants to reveal to you."[68]

If you are still not sure what Jesus meant, take a stroll through Matthew 23 sometime. In His teaching to the crowds and disciples, Jesus called the Pharisees hypocrites, snakes, even a "brood of vipers." The sound bite that caught the ten-o'clock news was "You blind guides! You strain out a gnat but swallow a camel" (Matthew 23:24).

Have you ever felt that the politics and policies of education sometimes strain out the gnats, but you're expected to swallow the camel? Does it seem to you that policymakers, who are not in the trenches, are completely missing the point?

The Pharisees were the religious right, but they were dead wrong! Jesus came to get the Jews back on track. Jesus came to fulfill the law—to redefine, reinterpret the law—and He did just that in His Sermon on the Mount in Matthew 5, 6, and 7. He began His incredible "reteach" with the Beatitudes. *Read Matthew 5:3–12.*

Blessed are you who are spiritually poor—when you have made yourself, as
Oswald Chambers calls it, "broken bread and poured out wine"[69] for others.

---

[68] Blackaby, Henry and Richard. *Experiencing God Day by Day*, p. 309.
[69] Chambers, Oswald. *My Utmost for His Highest*, p.99.

Blessed are you who mourn and have beheld and experienced deep loss and suffering but also a depth of connection to God that was a landmark in your faith journey.

Blessed are you who have used gentleness, understanding, and patience when you could have used your strength or authority instead.

Blessed are you who hunger to stay right with God rather than yield to the incessant demands and "wisdom" of the world.

Blessed are you who stretch yourself to show mercy and do things for God's reasons and not for posturing or ulterior motives of your own.

Blessed are you who come with an open, childlike, unpretentious heart. God is there.

Blessed are you who take the time to make peace rather than just keep the peace.

Blessed are you when, in their ignorance or jealousy, people make fun of you or make your life harder for trying to stay right with God. In all these things, you will be blessed and filled and comforted, and you will experience the kingdom of heaven right here on earth.

These godly attitudes represent all kinds of situations we humans walk through and get mired in daily. The depth and authenticity of faith and emotions they elicit are not surface, not fun, but real. Therein lies the difference between the proud, empty façade of the Pharisees and those who know the depth of their poverty without a relationship to God. The good news Emmanuel (God with us) brought us is that God wants to really be with us, to be in relationship with us. It's not about the law; it's about relationship. It's not how "good" we are; it's how good God is.

- What about education? How have education laws and practices affected the student/teacher relationship?

_____

_____

_____

Jesus even had a mission statement. Don't you just love it? Even back in biblical times, they had mission statements; only Jesus's mission statement was proclaimed some seven hundred years before by the prophet Isaiah (Isaiah 61:1–2). It just "happened" to be the Torah scroll handed to Jesus to read when He was in His hometown, Nazareth. *Read Luke 4:16–21.*

Do you remember the game "Step on a Crack and Break Your Mother's Back"? It's a game you cannot win, just as the game the Pharisees were playing, "Keep the Myriad of Laws," was impossible to win.

The good news was to be preached to those who had no hope of keeping those laws and were imprisoned and bound by them. They would no longer be blind; they would no longer be prisoners of the law. Their spiritual eyes would be opened, and they would no longer be oppressed in their hopelessness. The year of the Lord's favor was and is *now*! "Today this scripture is fulfilled in your hearing." Let it be and AMEN!

How is God using this lesson to equip you? Record meaningful statements, ideas, and scriptures you may want to remember and use as He equips you for the task for which He is calling you.

_____

_____

_____

_____

_____

_____

_____

Disturb Us, Lord

Disturb us, Lord, when
We are too well pleased with ourselves,
When our dreams have come true
Because we have dreamed too little,
When we arrived safely
Because we sailed too close to the shore.
Disturb us, Lord, when
With the abundance of things we possess
We have lost our thirst
For the waters of life;
Having fallen in love with life,
We have ceased to dream of eternity
And in our efforts to build a new earth,
We have allowed our vision
Of the new Heaven to dim.
Disturb us, Lord, to dare more boldly,
To venture on wider seas
Where storms will show your mastery;
Where losing sight of land,
We shall find the stars.
We ask You to push back
The horizons of our hopes;
And to push into the future
In strength, courage, hope, and love.
—Sir Francis Drake

*http://www.worldprayers.org/archive/prayers/invocations/disturb_us_lord_when_we.html

Day 3
HOW TO LOVE THE UNLOVABLE

CHILDREN WERE BROUGHT TO JESUS TO BE BLESSED;
WHAT DO CHILDREN RECEIVE WHEN THEY COME TO YOU?

Read Luke 18:15–17.

• Visualize this scene with today's parents and children. How would it look?

_____

_____

_____

*D*ID YOUR SCENE HAVE WELL-MANNERED, contented children and patient, smiling parents as the usual pictures of this Bible story portray? Or did your scene reveal loud, wiggly, tactilely inquisitive children and pushy, annoyed parents, thus verifying the angst of the disciples' original actions? In your scene, was Jesus divinely peaceful, or was His halo a tad tilted and dimmed?

No doubt, one of the favorite Bible stories of teachers is Jesus welcoming the little children after He had rebuked the disciples' attempts to keep them from bothering Him. He announced, "It is to such as these that the kingdom of God belongs. Truly I tell you, whoever does not receive the kingdom of God as a little child will never enter it."[70] HarperCollins commentary notes, "The qualities of openness, low status, and no claim to achievement characterize the *little child.*"

Again, Jesus turned traditional thinking upside down. Instead of pious, self-righteous, "law-full" Jews being first in line into the kingdom of God, Jesus was saying those with no outstanding knowledge or practice of the law and those lowest in social rank were fit for God's kingdom. No matter what station in life or accumulation of religious knowledge, the heart of the matter is our heart—is it open and seeking? Or is it full of ourselves and welded shut? Do we come to God as Father, Provider? Or do we merely ask God's blessings on our self-conceived plans?

Further, Jesus upset the Jewish "pecking order." Righteous Jewish men were considered exemplary, and Jewish men were recognized, but women, children, Gentiles, foreigners, and

---

[70] HarperCollins, p. 1,995. Luke 18:16–17.

slaves were of little account in Jesus's day. William Barclay gave an example: "Sabbath Law, for instance, lay it down that if, on the Sabbath, a wall should collapse on a passer-by, enough may be cleared to see whether the injured man is Jew or Gentile. If he is a Jew he may be rescued; if a Gentile he must be left to suffer."

Yes, it does seem cruel by today's standards, but every time one unfolds the newspaper, bias and heartlessness slap us in the face. And we wonder why bullying is so evident in our society? Bullying is age-old. *Read Luke 10:25–28.*

Yes, the Master Teacher permitted "cliff notes." Bottom line to all the hundreds of laws: Love God more than anything, and love your neighbor as yourself. Matthew says, "All the Law and the Prophets hang on these two commandments."[71]

- How do you interpret "neighbor"?

_____

_____

_____

Read Luke 10:29–37.

Amid the "Hatfield-McCoy" relationship between the Jews and Samaritans, Jesus very clearly painted a picture of neighbor: anyone in need of help, no matter their background or status. Again, this was revolutionary to devout Jews and revolting as well. The traveler was plainly foolish for journeying on this road alone. In their "eye for an eye" society, Jesus taught mercy and grace in this parable, help over hypocrisy.

How *do* you love your neighbor? Jesus tells us in Matthew 7:12 and Luke 6:31, "Do to others as you would have them do to you." Those of us who are long in the teaching tooth, remember that many students used to know the Golden Rule, as it was called. As of late, very few in the whole school know of this precious teaching. Yes, it is such an important teaching that character building curricula have secularized it, but the same curricula has yet to cultivate the kingdom of God.

As we visualized our present-day scenario of Jesus and the children, we would love for Jesus to jump up and quote Proverbs 13:24—"He who spares the rod hates his son, but he who loves him is careful to discipline him"—but He would not. We would want Him to calm the storm of squirm and noise—just a little miracle to zap some goodness into the kids—but He would not. He would touch them and bless them and perfectly love them.

Teachers, today's parents are bringing you the best they have. Some of their children are quiet and well mannered, some are anxious and shy, some are very bright and ready to learn, while other children are in a raging storm. Some don't know boundaries because they don't have boundaries or parenting. Maybe the parents are on a dangerous road of their own making, or they are paddling as fast as they can to stay afloat, but they've come to you bringing

---

[71] Matthew 22:40.

their children to be blessed and made better. We receive their children and try to connect with them. More and more, however, children are testing teachers' love and sincerity before students will trust and try.

How do we love them when they are unlovable? We have no idea what children or parents have been through in their lives, so first, we must not judge. Matthew 7:1–2 says, "DO NOT judge, or you too will be judged. For in the same way you judge others, you will be judged, and with the measure you use, it will be measured to you." Our culture is especially fond of name-calling and labeling. Judging others is a subtle form of bullying, for it involves a power differential.[72] If we are condescending or mentally making fun of our fellow man, we are not truly loving them, and no matter how incorrigible they are, our mental belittling will not be pleasing to God.

Second, we must show respect, for we are all made in the image of God. Jesus dealt with many unlovable people throughout His ministry—lepers, haughty Pharisees, the woman caught in adultery, tax collectors, women of questionable pasts—and He treated each one with respect despite their sin and shame. Practicing respect and manners used to be a given, but it's not so in society today. Seek to find and affirm special attributes in each person, for God has placed them there.

Third, God is fully aware who those difficult-to-love people are and where they have come from; He's also aware of "Whose you are and Whom you serve."[73] Share with Him in prayer how hard it is to deal with them and lift them up to your Father in prayer. Soak up His patience and compassion and gentleness.

Finally, the Master Teacher was a servant. *Read John 13:4–17.* "Do you understand what I have done for you?" The shocked disciples were dumbfounded, for washing feet was one of the most degrading acts a servant would do. "You call me 'Teacher' and 'Lord,' and rightly so, for that is what I am. Now that I, your Lord and Teacher, have washed your feet, you also should wash one another's feet." Our Lord Jesus demonstrated His love by serving His disciples/students. "I have set you an example that you should do as I have done for you." We are all entitled to love; we should not be too entitled to serve.

- Think of someone in your school environment with whom you find it's hard to deal. How could you employ these steps with them?

  _____

  _____

  _____

These steps—not judging, respect, prayer, and serving—won't be found in any teaching-methods class, but these are methods used by the Master Teacher. Just as Jesus is our example, we preach volumes to our students and colleagues by what we do. An environment of respect

---

[72] Hymel, Shelly and Susan Swearer. "Bullying: An Age-old Problem That Needs New Solutions," http://www.education.com/reference/article/bullying-about-power-and-abuse-of-power/.

[73] Chambers, Oswald. *My Utmost for His Highest*, p. 30, February 11.

and helping one another increases the worth of each individual. What's more, it can heal scars inflicted by others. As trite as it is, you may be as close as some kids come to Jesus. Encounters with Jesus changed many a life. Go and do likewise.

How is God using this lesson to equip you? Record meaningful statements, ideas, and scriptures you may want to remember and use as He equips you for the task for which He is calling you.

Day 4
JESUS HAD TO GET AWAY FROM THE PECKING TOO

JESUS FED THE MULTITUDES; ARE MULTITUDES FEEDING ON YOU?

*T*EACHING SCHOOL IS LIKE GETTING pecked to death by a chicken. You've been there. Dealing with children, parents, colleagues, and administration with their bombardment of questions, comments, wants, and needs all day long leaves one exhausted and spent at the end of the day. Positive relationships with all these folks are important, as are the hundreds of decisions a teacher makes daily that impact the lives of so many people. At the day's end, reserves of civility can run pretty low. Children of teachers who survive into adulthood know to give their teaching parent a little decompression time after school before they too commence with the pecking.

Jesus also had to withdraw. He had the Pharisees pecking him with their questions meant to trap Him. He had those with sickness and infirmities following Him. There were curiosity-seekers ready to see a miracle and get a free meal, along with others who were genuinely drawn by His testament of the good news. Even divine civility can run thin, and Jesus made time to get away.

Mark 1:35 (NRSV) reports that, "In the morning, while it was still very dark, he got up and went out to a deserted place, and there he prayed." Luke 6:12-13 (NRSV) discloses, "Now during those days he went out to the mountain to pray; and he spent the night in prayer to God. And when day came, he called his disciples and chose twelve of them." Jesus prayed early in the morning, and He prayed into the night. He prayed before big decisions and during crises, but it's clear that He regularly spent time in prayer as is noted by many references to Jesus withdrawing to pray throughout the Gospels.

Jesus was the Son of God, but apparently, the Son of Man part of Him had need of connection to His Father. If Jesus had that need, how much more do we need to connect with our Father in prayer?

• Do you have a regular time apart with God?

_____

_____

_____

- Read *Matthew 6:5–15* and *Luke 11:1–13*, and note some things that are important to remember when you pray:

_____

_____

_____

If "your Father knows what you need before you ask him" (Matthew 6:8 NRSV), then why pray? Oswald Chambers says, "Prayer is the way the life of God is nourished. Our ordinary views of prayer are not found in the New Testament. We look upon prayer as a means of getting things for ourselves; the Bible idea of prayer is that we may get to know God Himself." Can there be any viable relationship if one spends no time with the other? "It is not so true that 'prayer changes things' as that prayer changes *me* and I change things."[74]

Matthew also notes that we must forgive others, for God knows the soul bias and toxicity that is produced when we hold grudges and hurt deep in our hearts. God wants us, warts and all. He will sweep out our sin if we will sweep out our perceived hurts at the hands of others.

In Luke, Jesus taught persistence in prayer. We are to ask, seek, and knock persistently, for just as we seek the best for our children, so much more will God bless those who keep coming to Him with open, seeking, and pure hearts. We can't be pure in and of ourselves, for we are naturally tainted with selfishness and independence; it is only in our bowing to God in prayer, acknowledging His sovereignty, that our hearts are humbled and dependent on Him and His will. "Beware of refusing to go to the funeral of your own independence."

Libraries of books have been written about how to connect to God in prayer. There is no "one size fits all" formula for time devoted to God. As we all have different learning styles, we must develop our own devotional practices exploring time, place, methods, and materials. There are many great daily devotional books and magazines available providing scripture and inspirational reading that springboard thoughts and questions to discuss with your Father. Journaling is also a great way to connect and can provide a faith history as well. The important thing is to get free of the worldly screams of the urgent to do the truly important –just start by being real before God.

When Jesus's heard of the death of John the Baptist, "He withdrew from there in a boat to a deserted place by himself," but the crowds followed Him. Jesus was grieved and needed some space, but instead, He patiently taught "Thinking Out of the Box 101" to His disciples by feeding a crowd of five thousand men plus all the women and children (Matthew 14:13-20 NRSV). Later Jesus sent His disciples ahead in the boat, "And after he had dismissed the crowds, he went up the mountain by himself to pray." Jesus was bereft and probably very tired of human pecking, so He climbed up the mountain and connected with the Source and spent most of the night in prayer.

How many times was Jesus discouraged because, despite the reteach and remediation, the disciples just didn't "get it"? God stretched Jesus just as He may be stretching you. You may have heard it said that "God won't give us more than we can handle." That's not true. God will never give us more than *He* can handle. It's not about being godly—it's about being God's.

"It was said of Jesus—'He shall not fail nor be discouraged,' because He never worked from

---

[74] Chambers, Oswald. *My Utmost for His Highest*, p. 177.

His own individual standpoint but always from the standpoint of His Father, and we have to learn to do the same. Spiritual truth is learned by atmosphere, not by intellectual reasoning. God's Spirit alters the atmosphere of our way of looking at things, and things begin to be possible which never were possible before. Getting into the stride of God means nothing less than union with Himself," counsels Chambers.

- Comedians tell us, "As long as there are pop quizzes, there will be prayer in school." Does your heart and mind call upon God during your day at school?

  _____

  _____

  _____

- Just as you do lesson plans in preparation for your day, do you pray in preparation for the school day?

  _____

  _____

  _____

We all have different reference points when it comes to our idea of "father"—some have wonderful memories, some might shudder, while others have no memories at all. The fact is we are princesses and princes. We are *beloved* children of the King of the universe, Who, unlike our earthly father, is never absent or too busy to talk with us and give us His wisdom, grace, and guidance.

And isn't it great to have such an amazing big brother as Jesus to look up to? Unlike many earthly big brothers, He doesn't mind us hanging around and bothering Him. He so sounds and acts like Dad. "Jesus declared, 'I am the bread of life. He who comes to me will never go hungry, and he who believes in me will never be thirsty'" (John 6:35 NRSV). If the multitudes are feeding on you, then make time to come and be filled.

How is God using this lesson to equip you? Record meaningful statements, ideas, and scriptures you may want to remember and use as He equips you for the task for which He is calling you.

_____

_____

_____

_____

_____

Day 5

GOD'S PRESENCE CAN BALANCE
THE SEESAW YOU'RE ON

BALANCE IN THE "UPS AND DOWNS" OF LIFE

*R*EMEMBER THE "UNOFFICIAL" RULES FOR the playground seesaw? Always seesaw with a partner who is about your size. Choose someone you can trust—someone who won't bump down hard when your end goes up so you're launched into space. Also, you want to make sure your partner tells you when they're ready to get off so you don't come crashing down unexpectedly.

Life can be a seesaw ride, and balance plays a big part of it. Sometimes you are dangling and dancing in the air when you're dealing with something weighty. At times you receive a jolt, while every once in a while, you come crashing down when things seemed to be going so well. Does balancing school, family, church, and other things in your life leave you hanging on for dear life? *Read Luke 10:38–42.*

Mary was sitting at Jesus's feet listening, learning, and fellowshipping with Him, while Martha was all up in the air, dangling in exasperation. According to Henry and Richard Blackaby, "Martha loved Jesus dearly … [but she] spent so much time serving Jesus that she had no time to enjoy His company or to get to know Him better. The harder Martha worked, the more frustrated she became with her sister Mary … Martha's service, though it started out with gladness, deteriorated into resentment and envy … [W]hen your activity consumes your time and energies so that you have no time for Him, you have become too busy! … Jesus taught that your highest priority must be your relationship with Him. If anything detracts you from that relationship, that activity is not from God."[75]

Calm down all you type-A Marthas. Homes, schools, businesses, and churches could not run without you—the world needs Marthas! But how many times have you heard, "Don't work harder, work smarter"? It's about being efficient—Marthas love efficiency! Jesus knows the answer before we utter the question. He knows our frustration and resentment long before we realize it. As we spend time with Jesus in His Word and seek His perspective in our lives, we will be able to untangle the web of distractions and focus on what is important. "Be still and know that I am God," says Psalm 46:10.

How many of you are feeling guilty reading this instead of grading papers? Or spending time with your husband or children? Or dealing with the mountain of dirty clothes? Or … or … or … Is the prince of this world bombarding you with distraction after distraction as he did Martha?

---

[75] Blackaby, Henry and Richard. *Experiencing God Day by Day*, p. 337.

Listen to Jesus: "You are worried and upset about many things, but only one thing is needed. Mary has chosen what is better ..." *You* have chosen what is better.

Jesus has *many* things to tell you. Matthew, Mark, Luke, and John are filled with His word, God's word. "Christianity is not a set of teachings to understand. It is a Person to follow."[76] You are not cramming for an exam by rote memory; you are trying to apply and incorporate Jesus's teachings into your life so others will see the "family resemblance" and know that you have been with Jesus.

- Can you think of someone in your life to whom you were drawn because you could see their resemblance to Jesus and His teachings? Who and why?

  _____

  _____

  _____

- Could you be that person in your school? Or workplace?

  _____

  _____

  _____

Many states have comprehensive standardized testing of students over essential grade level teaching points. School districts put tons of pressure on teachers concerning these tests, and careers sometimes hang in the balance. The few days right before the testing are stressful as teachers feverishly shore up weak areas and reinforce important points.

The Master Teacher was experiencing the same pressure, for it was the Passover feast, and Jesus had only a few hours left to prepare the disciples for their big test early in the morning. Jesus already knew that one of the disciples would fail, since Judas had left to betray Him. Peter was demonstrating impulsivity and overconfidence, and that concerned Jesus, for his confidence would soon turn to panic and fear (John 13:36–38). Even reliable Philip isn't "getting it." You can hear a hint of exasperation in Jesus's voice as He says to him, "Don't you know me, Philip, even after I have been among you such a long time?" (John 14:10)

When teachers want to really stress a point, they will say the same thing in several different ways. *Read* the Master Teacher's words reinforcing important points before the testing in *John 14:6–15:17.*

- What are some of the main points Jesus makes in these verses that were important for the disciples and are important for us?

  _____

  _____

  _____

---

[76] Ibid., p. 25.

"I am the way and the truth and the life. No one comes to the Father except through me" (John 14:6). "Whoever has seen me has seen the Father" (John 14:9). "If you love me, you will obey what I command. And I will ask the Father, and he will give you another Counselor to be with you forever—the Spirit of truth" (John 14:15–17). "I am the vine; you are the branches. If a man remains [abides] in me and I in him, he will bear much fruit; apart from me you can do nothing" (John 15:5). Jesus made it abundantly clear the night He was arrested that the disciples should remember the truths He taught. They must trust Him and remain faithful to Him by obedience to those truths and not be distracted by all that would go on in the next few days. "Just as a spinning ballerina must keep returning her eyes to a given point to maintain her balance, so you must keep returning your focus to Me."[77] Remain … remain … stay balanced.

Schools are goal-driven, results-oriented organizations. They are too often the source of anxiety in their demands for positive outcomes and too often leave teachers spinning in their efforts. Do you feel driven in your efforts to produce? It's not about spinning, it's about abiding; it's not about effort alone, it's about relationship with the Vine, Jesus.

When a precious loved one dies, we carry that person in our hearts through our memories of them. Filed away in our brains are the essence of who they were in their thought, word, and deed. Many times our lives are colored by their profound influence on us because of the time we spent with them.

That's the way it is with the Word of God spoken by Jesus in the Gospels. The more time you spend with Jesus, the more His Holy Spirit will be able to teach you and have you recall the teaching as you have need. Testing in this life is inevitable, but we are not alone in this. The Spirit of God stands ready to uphold us in this dizzy seesaw ride. He can be in your heart and in your mind and as close as your breath. In Jesus and in His Word, we will find our balance.

Sit still, my children! Just sit calmly still!
Nor deem these days—these waiting days—as ill!
The One who loves you best, who plans your way,
Has not forgotten your great need today!
And, if He waits, it's sure He waits to prove
To you, His tender child, His heart's deep love.

Sit still, my children! Just sit calmly still!
You greatly long to know your dear Lord's will!
While anxious thoughts would almost steal their way
Corrodingly within, because of His delay—
Persuade yourself in simple faith to rest
That He, who knows and loves, will do the best.

---

[77] Young, Sarah. *Jesus Calling*, p. 120.

Sit still, my children! Just sit calmly still!
Nor move one step, not even one, until
His way has opened. Then, ah then, how sweet!
How glad your heart, and then how swift your feet,
Your inner being then, ah then, how strong!
And waiting days not counted then too long.

Sit still, my daughter! Just sit calmly still!
What higher service could you for Him fill?
It's hard! Ah yes! But choicest things must cost!
For lack of losing all how much is lost!
It's hard, it's true! But then—He gives you grace
To count the hardest spot the sweetest place.

—J. Danson Smith[78]

How is God using this lesson to equip you? Record meaningful statements, ideas, and scriptures you may want to remember and use as He equips you for task for which He is calling you.

_____

_____

_____

_____

_____

_____

_____

---

[78] *Streams in the Desert*, pp. 62–63.

Group Questions for Jesus Was Called

- William Barclay's view in Day 1 was that true Christianity was "bound to carry out" a moral, social, and economic revolution. Is the Bible out of touch with the times, or are our times out of touch with the intent of the Gospels? How do these three "revolutions" affect your classroom/work situation? If they don't, then should they?

- "If sin was not keeping all the Jewish laws, then ordinary Jews must have felt enchained to sin and hopelessness." Do you have a better sense now of just how good the "good news" Jesus preached was to ordinary Jews and Gentiles? What about the people of today? Do you think they are as entrenched in sin and hopelessness as in Jesus's times?

- In Day 2, Henry and Richard Blackaby define a Pharisee as someone who does not have a teachable spirit. How do you deal with people who fit this description? Do you know or work with educational Pharisees?

- Reread the last paragraph of Day 3. Develop an understanding of what "go and do likewise" would involve.

- Day 4 speaks to the importance of prayer and "being real before God." How are you restored, filled, and rested? Share some of your devotional practices.

- Consider the story of Mary and Martha in Day 5. What does this story teach us about distractions, peace, focus, and even resolving conflict? When you are spinning in fretful distraction, what reminds you to "be still" and focus on "abiding" and "remaining" in God?

Paul Was Called

WEEK 5

Day 1

PAUL TEACHES ABOUT GRACE

MY MIND'S MADE UP; DON'T CONFUSE ME WITH THE FACTS

IT WASN'T HIS MOTHER'S LACK of trying to lay the groundwork for a good Christian life. Elizabeth Newton could very well have made a difference in her son's life if she had lived past his seventh birthday (1732), but between a distant sea captain father and unsuccessful stints with his stepmother and boarding school, eleven-year-old John decided to set sail. He yearned for his mother's love and kept trying to remember bits of scripture she taught him, but his remembrances of a judgmental God and the lure of the debaucheries in the life of a sailor proved to him he would never measure up, so he gave up trying. Instead, he challenged himself to invent new ways of offending the name and character of God that would make the most contemptuous sailor recoil and stiffen.

Saul, on the other hand, was a young man with everything going for him: His supportive family was Jewish, and he was "of the tribe of Benjamin, a Hebrew of Hebrews; in regard to the law, a Pharisee."[79] He had sat at the feet of the highly esteemed rabbi, Gamaliel, so his education and pedigree were impeccable. This zealous young man was eager to make a name for himself, so as a witness to the "blasphemies" of Stephen and his subsequent stoning,[80] Saul declared a personal war against the followers of Jesus. According to Acts 8:3, "Saul began to destroy the church. Going from house to house, he dragged off men and women and put them in prison." His righteousness as a Jew, and his hatred for the people who were trying to undermine everything he knew as holy prompted him to go to the high priest and procure letters of authorization to capture and imprison those treacherous dissidents.

They didn't know it, but the lives of these two men were on a collision course with grace. In fact, they were already neck deep in what John Wesley called "prevenient grace," the grace that "comes before." "Wesley believed that God places a little spark of divine grace within us"[81] to draw us to Him. We may reject Him, in our feelings of unworthiness, as Newton did, or reject Him in our self-righteousness, as Saul did, but neither man knew how much God longed for them to turn to Him. Nor did they realize how much they needed God. Saint Augustine spoke of our heart being restless until it rests in God.

---

[79] Philippians 3:5.
[80] Acts 7.
[81] http://gbgm-umc.org/umw/wesley/walk.stm.

- Have you ever felt the restlessness of which Saint Augustine spoke?

_____

_____

_____

Many times we are blind to the events in our lives drawing us toward God, but we will feel a restlessness or emptiness (Newton). This restlessness can also manifest itself in our becoming driven toward what we perceive as good but is dissatisfying in effect (Paul). That emptiness or dissatisfaction is God's prevenient grace beckoning us to Him.

As a "Hebrew of Hebrews," Saul's life was centered on the Mosaic law. As a student of Gamaliel, surely he heard the respected rabbi's advice concerning the followers of Jesus. In Acts 5:38–39, Gamaliel said, "Leave these men alone! Let them go! For if their purpose or activity is of human origin, it will fail. But if it is from God, you will not be able to stop these men; you will only find yourselves fighting against God."

In Acts 6, Stephen, a brother chosen by the apostles who was "full of God's grace and power," ministered so miraculously that some plotted against him and dragged him before the Sanhedrin (Acts 7). The crux of Stephen's long speech was that Israel has historically resisted God's plan and the men who presented it. Stephen finally said to them, "You stiff-necked people, with uncircumcised hearts and ears! You are just like your fathers: You always resist the Holy Spirit!" (Acts 7:51)

Saul fought tooth and nail to preserve his ancestral way of life and refused to listen to the wise rabbi or to the spirit-filled testimony of Stephen. His mindset was "My mind is made up—don't confuse me with the facts!" It's really frustrating when you work for or with stubborn, hard-hearted people who are not hard of hearing but are hard of listening. You'd just like God to zap them, wouldn't you? He did just that to Saul.

Read Acts 9:1–22.

Saul's conversion was immediate. He was confronted by the Lord Jesus, and he quite literally "made a U-ie" right there on the Damascus road. With John Newton, however, it took two conversion experiences. During a disastrous storm at sea, he cried to God and was saved from the storm, but he soon returned to his old ways. On his next voyage, he contracted a fever and in his weakness, again called to God, but this time he offered himself up to the will of God. Instead of the legalistic, judgmental, gotcha-God Newton had known, he realized that in His love, God gave His own Son to hang on the cross nailed there by Newton's own sins. Only then did he realize he had been made "right" with God. He was forgiven and at peace with God.

In Romans 3:21–24, Paul wrote, "A righteousness from God, apart from the law has been made known … This righteousness from God comes through faith in Jesus Christ to all who believe … for all have sinned and fall short of the glory of God, and are justified freely by his grace through the redemption that came by Christ Jesus." Also, Romans 5:1, 2 says, "Therefore, since we have been justified through faith, we have peace with God through our Lord Jesus Christ, through whom we have gained access by faith into this grace in which we now stand." When we have accepted that Christ died for our sins, God has deemed us righteous, and we are justified in His eyes. That's "justifying grace."

- "The essence of salvation is an about-face from self-centeredness to God-centeredness."[82] Was your conversion experience (your about-face) a sudden turn-around like Paul? Or was it a haltingly slower turn like Newton's? Or are you still being pursued and wooed by God?

_____

_____

_____

After we have been made right with God through our professed faith in Jesus, we move into "sanctifying grace," in which God is "progressively separating a believer from sin to Himself and transforming his total life experience toward holiness and purity."[83] Simply put, it is God-centeredness, aligning ourselves with God, and, as Oswald Chambers says, being "kept by the power of God."[84]

Saul was undoubtedly called by God. To Ananias, God said, "This man is my chosen instrument to carry my name before the Gentiles and their kings and before the people of Israel" (Acts 9:15).

- Think about Saul's qualifications. Why do you think God chose him to take His message to the Gentiles and the Jewish people?

_____

_____

_____

Paul* was well educated. He could read and write, he was well trained in the Jewish law and history, and yet he was young enough to be able to travel extensively spreading the Gospel. Paul was zealous and unquestionably single-minded when it came to his faith. God undoubtedly saw those things in him and more. Can't you just imagine a powwow up in heaven between God and Jesus about who would carry the Gospel into the world? Can't you just hear them chuckle and then burst into roaring laughter when they decided to tap Saul to be their man? Who says God doesn't have a sense of humor? It would just take a mega dose of grace.

Heroic Ananias obeyed God and went to Saul, despite the fact that Saul was a persecutor of Christians and his sworn enemy. "Brother Saul," Ananias declared, "the Lord—Jesus, who appeared to you on the road … has sent me so that you may see again and be filled with the Holy Spirit."

"No single event, apart from the Christ-event itself, has proved so determinant for the course of Christian history as the conversion and commissioning of Paul … With no conscious preparation, Paul found himself instantaneously compelled by what he saw and heard to acknowledge that Jesus of Nazareth, the crucified one, was alive after his passion, vindicated and exalted by God,

---

* Saul (Hebrew name); Paul (Anglicized Roman name).

[82] Blackaby, Henry and Richard. *Experiencing God Day by Day*, p. 50.

[83] Walvoord and Zuck. *The Bible Knowledge Commentary*, p. 462.

[84] Chambers, Oswald. *My Utmost for His Highest*, p. 149.

and was now conscripting him into his service ... Paul's experience ... involved the intelligent and deliberate surrender of his will to the risen Christ who had appeared to him—the risen Christ who, from this time on, displaced the law as the center of Paul's life and thought."[85]

While Saul's learning curve in sanctifying grace went straight up, John Newton's was a bumpy climb. After Newton's conversion, he began reading and growing as a Christian during his voyages as the captain of a ship—a slave ship. Finally, a serious illness caused him give up his commission as a captain and find other work. Sixteen years after his conversion experiences, he was ordained as a minister and even began to write hymns. His most famous hymn was entitled "Faith's Review and Expectation,"[86] but it is better known by the first two words of the hymn:

Amazing grace! How sweet the sound
That saved a wretch like me!
I once was lost, but now am found;
Was blind, but now I see.

'Twas grace that taught my heart to fear,
And grace my fears relieved;
How precious did that grace appear
The hour I first believed.

Through many dangers, toils and snares,
I have already come;
'Tis grace hath brought me safe thus far,
And grace will lead me home.

The Lord has promised good to me,
His word my hope secures;
He will my shield and portion be,
As long as life endures.

Yea, when this flesh and heart shall fail,
And mortal life shall cease,
I shall possess, within the veil,
A life of joy and peace.

The world shall soon dissolve like snow,
The sun refuse to shine;
But God, who called me here below,
Shall be forever mine.

---

[85] Bruce, F. F. *PAUL Apostle of the Heart Set Free*, pp. 75–76.
[86] Morgan, Robert. *Then Sings My Soul*, p. 79.

When we've been there ten thousand years,
Bright shining as the sun,
We've no less days to sing God's praise
Than when we'd first begun.

John Newton and Paul are two extremes in their stories of grace. Our stories probably fall somewhere in between these, but the grace it took to get us there is the same: the grace that "wooed" you to God, the grace that opened your eyes to see Jesus's sacrifice for you nailed there by all our sins, and finally, the grace that fosters and nurtures your walk with God through God's Holy Spirit. It is *amazing*.

JUSTICE is …
Getting what we deserve.

MERCY is …
Not getting what we deserve.

GRACE is …
Getting what we don't deserve.[87]

How is God using this lesson to equip you? Record meaningful statements, ideas, and scriptures you may want to remember and use as He equips you for the task for which He is calling you.

_____

_____

_____

_____

_____

_____

_____

---

[87] Author unknown, but Bill Sewell used it often and well.

Day 2

WE ARE TRANSFORMED BY LOVE

TRANSFORMED: FROM SAUL, ROBOT PHARISEE, TO PAUL, MEGA-MISSIONARY AND THEOLOGICAL TITAN

*W*HY DO YOU THINK LITTLE boys are so attracted to toys called Transformers? Is it because they get bored with one toy and one play scenario and they can switch to a "different" toy and venue of action? It changes, for example, from a spaceship or motorcycle or airplane to a super action figure. Is it about mechanics? Is it about power or speed? Is it about the element of surprise? Or is it about control?

Saul was the much-dreaded Robot Pharisee, gathering, arresting, imprisoning. The followers of Jesus were no match for him; he was impervious to their "blasphemous practices." Enter the Lord, who has another use for Saul—"This man is my chosen instrument to carry my name before the Gentiles and their kings and before the people of Israel" (Acts 9:15). Saul was chosen, but how was this Robot Pharisee transformed for this task?

Read Acts 9:17.

- What did Ananias do to equip Saul?

_____

_____

_____

Let's take a step back and look at some of the rich irony at play here. Saul's namesake, King Saul, twice disobeyed God, and the Spirit of God "departed from Saul" (1 Samuel 16:14). From that time on, Saul was possessed with jealousy and tried to hunt down and kill David, who had been anointed with the Spirit of the Lord. King Saul lost the Holy Spirit; David, anointed by God, received it. Over a thousand years later, Saul persecuted the "Son of David's" followers, and then *he* was filled with the Holy Spirit. In short, King Saul lost the Holy Spirit and then persecuted David. Saul persecuted Christ's followers and *then* received the Holy Spirit. God has been playing "transformers" for a long time.

Ananias placed his hands on Saul and said, "Brother Saul, the Lord—Jesus, who appeared to you on the road as you were coming here—has sent me so that you may see again and be filled with the Holy Spirit" (Acts 9:17). There it is: Saul was transformed and equipped by the Holy Spirit. He was a new creation. In fact, instead of rounding up the Christians to imprison them, in Acts 9:20, he "at once began to preach in the synagogues that Jesus is the Son of God." Verse

22 reports, "Yet Saul grew more and more powerful and baffled the Jews living in Damascus by proving that Jesus is the Christ."

Think about it. This is what test-taking students have been praying for almost two thousand years—that God would just zap the solution right into their brains, that the scales would fall from their eyes, and they would be able to see the answers! But Paul had, in fact, spent many years studying. Since Paul and Jesus were fairly close in age, perhaps he studied under rabbis who squirmed at the questioning of the twelve-year-old Jesus. Paul had knowledge of the law and the prophets. So did Jesus.

When Jesus appeared to the disciples on the road to Emmaus after His resurrection, Luke 24:27 confirms that "beginning with Moses and all the Prophets, he explained to them what was said in all the scriptures concerning himself." While Paul would have had that same background in the knowledge of the law and the prophets, the Holy Spirit simply but profoundly opened his eyes to its fulfillment in Jesus Christ. In Christ, all the pieces fell into place, and from that moment on, his identification with Christ was complete—"I no longer live, but Christ lives in me" (Galatians 2:20). The zeal that drove the Hebrew Saul toward persecution of Christians was now couched in Paul, the "bondslave" of the risen Christ, who was constrained to preach the message of Christ to the ends of the earth.

The esteemed Bible scholar F. F. Bruce recognized that "Paul's understanding of God is completely in line with Jesus' teaching,"[88] which, again, is the work of the Holy Spirit. This is affirmed in Galatians 1:11, when Paul said, "I did not receive [the Gospel] from any man, nor was I taught it; rather, I received it by revelation from Jesus Christ." Also, 1 Corinthians 2:16 quotes Isaiah, "For who has known the mind of the Lord so as to instruct him?" And then Paul asserts, "But we have the mind of Christ."

The influence of Christ on Paul's teaching and doctrine is very evident. According to *The Revell Bible Dictionary*, "Paul, more than any other, presents a distinctive Christian theology, one that is consistent with and yet supplants the theology of the Old Testament."[89] Paul "got it" about what Jesus tried to teach before and after the cross, and he was able to expound upon Christ's teaching in his own ministry and remain true to the Word. But especially effective were the letters he wrote to the churches he established. Just as Christ was the Good Shepherd, Paul was a good shepherd to his flock and to us centuries later.

During Jesus's ministry, He summarized Jewish law into two commandments: Love God and love your neighbor. To further explain love for neighbor, He told the parable of the Good Samaritan to His Jewish audience. Paul, in ministry to his church in Corinth, faced a very diverse population and a citizenry that was generally materialistic and vulgar. To exemplify love in this culture, Paul gave them a list of what love is and is not, topped by his declaration that, "Love never fails."

Read 1 Corinthians 13 with particular attention to 13:4–7. (Note: Translations will differ as to wording and number.)

---

[88] Bruce, F. F. *Paul: Apostle of the Heart Set Free*, p. 19.
[89] *The Revell Bible Dictionary*, p. 761.

Love is …		Love is not …	
•		•	
•		•	
•		•	
•		•	
•		•	
•		•	
•		•	

- Put a check by the points with which you don't usually have trouble. Place an arrow beside the points you still struggle with or a question mark if you are uncertain.
- Think back to the last strained encounter you had with someone. Jot down a few words to remind you what transpired.

_____

_____

_____

- Now go down the list and reflect on your response and your motives according to Paul's idea of love. What are your thoughts?

_____

_____

_____

Usually we hear this scripture at weddings, when the pastor reads it to perhaps the two most "in love" people in the room. We are, however, missing the best use of this scripture: 1 Corinthians 13:4–7 is a litmus test of all our daily actions and motives. As we reflect on our dealings with others, we can many times get past the first five or six on the list, but when we come nose-to-nose with the admonishment not to be self-seeking or to delete our files of past wrongs, we can get a little testy (easily angered?) about these "outdated" rules. Can we "rejoice in the truth" of who we've become? If you're breathing, you're probably convicted.

Then there are the last four qualities that love is *always* supposed to do: "[Love] always protects, always trusts, always hopes, always perseveres."[90] Do you feel as if you are being set up for failure here? But it's at this point, Paul says, "Love never fails."[91]

We know love fails. We have seen it shatter the children in our classroom as their parents fall out of love and fall into bitterness and hateful behavior. We see it down the hall when a colleague is ripped apart as their family dissolves. We may personally have felt the throes of anguish when

---

[90] 1 Corinthians 13:7.
[91] 1 Corinthians 13:8.

love, which we made a bedrock in our life, quaked and crumbled. In their single-mindedness about their ministries, neither Paul nor Jesus were married; does that disqualify them from speaking about love? Or are these statements speaking to ways of lending respect and dignity to all people—even well-worn spouses?

Just as the Ten Commandments had some laws dealing with our relationship with man and others dealing with our relationship with God, it is the same with the laws of love. The "always" qualities—trust, protect, hope, and persevere—are those that apply to our relationship to God. If we put all our trust and hope in a person, then they are god to us, especially if we protect this relationship and persevere in it. Oswald Chambers put it very well: "Our Lord trusted no man; yet He was never suspicious, never bitter, never in despair about any man, because He put God first in trust ... If I put my trust in human beings first, I will end in despairing of everyone."[92] Christ was not out to glorify Himself; He was out to glorify His Father God. In the same way, Paul was not in ministry to further his position or power; in fact, he considered himself dead to his old life, and his life was "hidden with Christ in God."

So if we are serious about following the Master Teacher, we, like Paul, must lay aside our selfish ideas of realizing all we want to be and let the perfect love of Christ guide us into all He has planned for us to be—not self-realization but Christ-realization. Paul's love has nothing to do with our emotions, our likes and dislikes. It's about overcoming our will, about being obedient and choosing God's will—the true heart of love.

We can *always* trust in the love of God. Paul says, "We also rejoice in our sufferings, because we know that suffering produces perseverance; perseverance, character; and character, hope. And hope does not disappoint us, because God has poured out his love into our hearts by the Holy Spirit, whom he has given us" (Romans 5:3–5). We can *always* hope, and we can *always* persevere in Him. He will *always* protect us. "And we know that in all things God works for the good of those who love him, who have been called according to his purpose," Paul assures us in Romans 8:28.

The question is, will we protect His life in us? Christ literally gave his body and blood for us on the cross, and Christ continues to give His body and blood for us in the form of a sacrament (Communion) of which Christians around the world still partake. In order to be useful in the kingdom and true to Christ's and Paul's vision of love, we have to be willing to be ground and squeezed into "broken bread and poured out wine" for others. We can only be nourishment for others as we forgo our selfish desires and cede our rights to ourselves over to the Holy Spirit. By dying to ourselves, we become alive in Christ. Then our lives, like Paul's, will be "hidden with Christ in God."

As 2 Corinthians 5:17 so magnificently declares, "Therefore, if anyone is in Christ, he is a new creation; the old has gone, the new has come!" We are transformed! Thanks be to God, for His love *never* fails!

---

[92] Chambers, Oswald. *My Utmost for His Highest*, p. 109.

Who shall separate us from the love of Christ?
Shall trouble or hardship or persecution or famine or nakedness or danger or sword?
As it is written: "For your sake we face death all day long;
We are considered as sheep to be slaughtered."
No
In all these things we are more than conquerors through him who loved us.
For I am convinced that neither death nor life, neither angels nor demons,
Neither the present nor the future, nor any powers,
Neither height nor depth, nor anything else in all creation,
Will be able to separate us from the love of God
That is in Christ Jesus our Lord.

Romans 8:35–39

Amen.

How is God using this lesson to equip you? Record meaningful statements, ideas, and scriptures you may want to remember and use as He equips you for the task for which He is calling you.

_____

_____

_____

_____

_____

_____

Day 3

USING OUR SPIRITUAL GIFTS TO FURTHER THE BODY OF CHRIST

STAFF DEVELOPMENT UNDER PRINCIPAL PAUL

In his *Meditation XVII*, John Donne wrote, "No man is an island, entire of itself; every man is a piece of the continent, a part of the main. If a clod be washed away by the sea, Europe is the less …: any man's death diminishes me, because I am involved in mankind, and therefore never send to know for whom the bells tolls; it tolls for thee." [93] At the risk of flunking an English literature essay question, John Donne, is indubitably saying that all mankind is connected in living and dying, even the clods are missed.

Paul's missive in *1 Corinthians 12:12–27* was very much related to Donne's quote. He spoke of the human body having many parts, each with individual tasks, which are joined together for the good of the whole. Read the passage and note how all believers are to be connected to one another.

Paul in this scripture is talking about the body of believers—how we are all different. Our DNA is different, and so are our life experiences, but as believers in Christ, we are called to unity. "You have one Master, one faith, one baptism, one God and Father of all, who rules over all, works through all, and is present in all. Everything you are and think and do is permeated with Oneness," says Ephesians 4:5–6. [94] It's easy to see that believers at our churches are "family," and even the body of believers as a whole are family, but can this apply to a school body as well?

The student-teacher was given some very sound advice by her supervising teacher: "The first person you want to make friends with on a new campus is the custodian. They always know what's going on at the campus," the supervising teacher reasoned, "and they're invaluable help for an abundance of things. Ours has helped me hang curtains and even jumped my dead car battery." The novice teacher didn't realize it, but that advice was straight from the pages of administrator Paul's Epistle. Those who may not stand out as an important part of the school body can make a huge difference in the climate and workings of a school.

Think of someone at your school who impacts your school climate for the better and may not receive the appreciation they deserve.

According to 1 Corinthians 12:4–6, in the Body of Christ, there are different spiritual gifts, different kinds of service, and different kinds of working, but the same Spirit, the same Lord, and the same God works in and through believers. The amazing news in 1 Corinthians 12:7 is this:

---

[93] http://www.online-literature.com/donne/409/.

[94] Peterson, Eugene. *The Message.*

"Now to each [believer] the manifestation of the Spirit is given for the common good." "Manifest" comes from the "Latin *manifestus,* literally, hit by the hand,"[95] so to each believer, the power of the Holy Spirit is "slapped on us," made evident or displayed in the form of a special expression or gift that we are to use not for our own personal gain but for the common good of the body of believers. The four scriptures in which Paul lists the gifts are below:

Spiritual Gifts

1 Corinthians 12:8–10: wisdom, knowledge, faith, healing, miracles, prophecy, discernment, tongues, interpretation of tongues

1 Corinthians 12:28: apostles, prophets, *teachers*, miracles, healing, helpers, administration, tongues

Ephesians 4:11: apostles, prophets, evangelists, pastors, *teachers*

Romans 12:6–8: gifts of prophecy, serving, *teaching*, encouraging, generosity, leadership, mercy

In three of the four scriptures, "teachers" or "teaching" is listed as a gift.

- Have you ever thought of teaching as a gift given to you by God's Holy Spirit?

  _____

  _____

  _____

- Besides teaching, do you think you have any other of these spiritual gifts?

  _____

  _____

  _____

- As you look at the list of spiritual gifts, think of the people on your campus, especially those who are doing *Called and Equipped* with you. Write beside a few of the gifts the name of someone on your campus in whom you have seen that gift.

  _____

  _____

  _____

Principal Paul had much experience working with people and reconciling them with the Body of Christ, but one does not have to read far into Paul's letters to the churches to see that he had his

---

[95] *Webster's Seventh New Collegiate Dictionary,* p. 514.

work cut out for him. In Galatia and Thessalonica, Paul was being discredited by false teachers, and he had to defend and reteach. In Corinth, they were quarreling about authority and greed; Paul had to unify them and teach them about love. In Rome, there was conflict between Jewish and Gentile believers, and he had to make big decisions reconciling both parties into the body of believers. Paul was no stranger to conflict, so his letters to the churches are a treasure trove of relationship do's and don'ts while staying true to the Body of Christ. A sampling of Paul's teaching about relationships follows:

"Therefore encourage one another and build up each other, as indeed you are doing" (1 Thessalonians 5:11).

"Do nothing out of selfish ambition or vain conceit, but in humility consider others better than yourselves" (Philippians 2:3).

"I appeal to you, brothers, in the name of our Lord Jesus Christ, that all of you agree with one another so that there may be no divisions among you and that you may be perfectly united in mind and thought" (1 Corinthians 1:10).

"Do not cause anyone to stumble, whether Jews, Greeks or the church of God— even as I try to please everybody in every way. For I am not seeking my own good but the good of many, so that they may be saved" (1 Corinthians 10:32-33).

"Share with God's people who are in need. Practice hospitality" (Romans 12:13).

"Accept him whose faith is weak, without passing judgment on disputable matters" (Romans 14:1).

"Let us therefore make every effort to do what leads to peace and to mutual edification" (Romans 14:19).

Much teaching, remediation, and reteach went into the pages of Paul's nine Epistles to the churches as he sought to shepherd and keep his flocks together as the Body of Christ. Again, what about our school bodies? Can we use Paul's teaching with our colleagues in school?

As a rule, teachers are strong personalities. They have to be in order to deal with so many students, parents, and staff all day long. Our colleagues can be a supportive body, or we can feel like an island. Oswald Chambers said, "Self-consciousness is the first thing that will upset the completeness of the life in God, and self-consciousness continually produces wrestling."[96] This self-conscious wrestling is usually manifested in comparing ourselves with others on our campus or workplace, and this is a double-edged sword.

If we compare to others favorably in our minds, we can become prideful, always striving to "stay on top" and above others. If we don't compare ourselves favorably with others, then we fear

---

[96] Chambers, Oswald. *My Utmost for His Highest*, p. 169.

they will find out how inadequate we are, so we pull away. Either way, we isolate ourselves. We become so preoccupied with "self" that in order to make us feel better about ourselves, we have to continually push or pull others down. If we feel above them, we push others down; if we feel below others, we pull them down. Either way, it will wreak havoc on the unity of the school body and on our physical bodies as well.

- Have you seen the effects of the struggles of pride and inadequacy on campus unity?

_____

_____

_____

This was not God's plan for us to be alone. Paul writes that Jesus "is the head of the body, the church; and he is the beginning and the firstborn from among the dead, so that in everything he might have the supremacy" (Colossians 1:18). As believers in Christ, He is our head, we are His body, His hands, and His feet. The Holy Spirit has a special gift for each of us to be used not for ourselves but for others, and *they* have special gifts too. We must recognize and appreciate the gifts of others. Remember: "The eye cannot say to the hand, 'I don't need you!' And the head cannot say to the feet, 'I don't need you!'" (1 Corinthians 12:21). When we quit being defensive and preoccupied with self, then we can open ourselves up to the Holy Spirit leading us to see the gifts of others and leading us toward unity and harmony.

If we use our spiritual gifts along with Paul's scriptural instruction, then it will be easy to get along with others in the school environment, right? Not so much. Teachers can't lock themselves in their rooms; we interact with others every day, all day long—students, parents, coworkers—and we are tested. In Galatians 5:16, Paul admonishes us to "live by the Spirit" and declares that "when the Holy Spirit controls our lives He will produce this kind of fruit in us: love, joy, peace, patience, kindness, goodness, faithfulness, gentleness and self-control" (Galatians 5:22–23, Living Bible).

- Have you seen evidence of the fruit of the Spirit in any of your colleagues? If so, who, and which fruit have you seen?

_____

_____

_____

Obviously, the supervising teacher valued her coworker, the custodian. Was she a Christian? Was the custodian a Christian? In the school environment, we don't always know, but what really does matter is how we treat others. As the hymn goes, "They will know we are Christians by our love." Did you notice the passages about the Body of Christ and spiritual gifts lead us right up to 1 Corinthians 13—the passage on love we studied in the previous lesson? The greatest gift is love. No matter the role to which we're appointed or what gifts we have been given or which fruits the Holy Spirit has grown in us, love cements us all together as the Body of Christ.

William Barclay said, "Christianity began with a group. The Christian faith is something which from the beginning had to be discovered and lived out in a fellowship … the very name Pharisee means 'the separated one'; the essence of Christianity was that it … presented [people] with the task of living with each other and for each other."[97]

As a pebble strikes the water and moves outward in concentric circles, our actions resonate and impact our circles of family, church, work/school, friends, and the Body of Christ as a whole. We are not alone. There is a body of believers who, though they aren't perfect, are called by Christ to care for one another in and through the Holy Spirit.

Come on—don't be the clod washed away by the sea. Be cared for in the Body of Christ.

How is God using this lesson to equip you? Record meaningful statements, ideas, and scriptures you may want to remember and use as He equips you for the task for which He is calling you.

_____

_____

_____

_____

_____

_____

_____

[97] Barclay, William. *Daily Study Bible Series: The Gospel of Mark* (Revised Edition). Louisville: Westminster John Knox Press, 1976, pp.73–74.

Day 4

GOD'S GRACE IS SUFFICIENT; THAT'S OUR HAPPILY-EVER-AFTER

Is "Happily Ever After" a Fairy Tale?

*D*O WE DO OUR CHILDREN a disservice by reading them fairy tales? The prince married the fair maiden, and they lived "happily ever after." Shouldn't it be more like the prince married the fair maiden, and they were happy for a while, but then they argued about the in-laws … Or the prince was pink-slipped by the king, and he was lying around in his royal socks and underwear all day … Or they had three stair-step children, and the princess was up to her eyeballs in diapers and not feeling very regal?

What is "happily ever after" anyway? Is it the perception that nothing disappointing, disturbing, or bad will ever happen to the "good" characters? That evil or the bad guys always lose? That after we get past this one bump in the road, life will be smooth sailing from here? Life is one long bumpy road, and the idea that we, as the main characters of our tales, are immune to life's pitfalls and that life is always fair is … well … a "fairy tale."

Some people think once they become a Christian, they will "be there," at happily-ever-after, and if they're a "good" Christian, life will always be fulfilling and wonderful. Paul would beg to differ. After Paul's "come to Jesus" meeting on the road to Damascus, "happily" and "wonderful" would not necessarily describe his life. In 2 Corinthians, Paul defended his ministry against "false apostles, deceitful workmen, masquerading as apostles of Christ. And no wonder, for Satan himself masquerades as an angel of light" (2 Corinthians 11:13–14). Paul felt he had to answer the boasts of the false teachers, although he felt foolish in "boasting" of or defending his ministry. Read *2 Corinthians 11:21b–30*.

- What are some of the bone-crushing obstacles/worries with which you are wrestling? What things are spoiling your "happily ever after"?

_____

_____

_____

_____

_____

_____

- Paul's weariness is palpable in these verses. "Then, besides all this, I have the constant worry of how the churches are getting along."[98] If you exchange the word "churches" for "students" in this verse, would it speak to the exhaustion you feel at the end of the day?

_____

_____

_____

_____

_____

_____

In verse 30, Paul states, "If I must boast, I will boast of the things that show my weakness." What a curious thing to say. *The Bible Knowledge Commentary* says, "Paul's boast was that his life was like that of Christ. As Jesus had been 'a Man of sorrows and familiar with suffering' (Isaiah 53:3), so had Paul."[99] For him to choose suffering would have been tragic and unacceptable, but suffering for and in the name of Jesus was completely worth it for Paul.

Paul spoke again of his weakness in the next chapter when he said, "There was given to me a thorn in my flesh, a messenger of Satan, to torment me" (2 Corinthians 12:7). "Countless explanations concerning the nature of his thorn in the flesh have been offered. They range from incessant temptation, dogged opponents, chronic maladies (such as ophthalmia, malaria, migraine headaches, and epilepsy), to a disability in speech."

Read 2 Corinthians 12:8–10.

Here is another of the amazing paradoxes of the Bible: When we are weak in and of ourselves, when we've done all we can do, when we've completely run out of gas, out of ideas, out of luck, out of hope, then we are in the perfect place for Christ's power to "rest on us." In his Christ-centered work, Paul delighted in those hard times, for when Paul was at the end of his human strength, wisdom, and power, it was just the beginning of Christ's—the perfect tag team. Child of God, stop and receive just the right word, just enough strength, just enough patience, just enough love; let the scales fall from your eyes and see the Spirit of God work in you and in your situation.

There are many things in our world that compete for our attention, some of which even vie for our faith. What is the "messenger of Satan" that torments you? There is so much disturbing news that batters us day in and day out: job cuts, the economy, finances, politics, weather and natural disasters, climate change, health problems, keeping up with technology, family problems. The list goes on and on in our ever-changing world. Satan is an expert at stirring up our fear until we are paralyzed and overwhelmed and hopeless.

This is precisely where Paul gets excited. "I delight in weaknesses, in insults, in hardships, in persecutions, in difficulties." For when Paul started getting fearful, he would remember his Partner, and he would tag Him. "For when I am weak, then I am strong" in Christ. Paraphrased from 2 Corinthians 6:4–10, Paul says, as God's partners we endure "troubles, hardships, and

---

[98] 2 Corinthians 11:28, Living Bible.
[99] Lowery, David K. *The Bible Knowledge Commentary*, p. 582.

distresses, beatings, imprisonments and riots, hard work, sleepless nights and hunger." But we also have "purity, understanding, patience and kindness"; we have "the Holy Spirit, sincere love, truthful speech and the power of God" … and weapons of righteousness in both hands. Their hearts ached, but at the same time, they rejoiced in the Lord. They were poor, but many were made rich through them. They owned nothing, but they possessed everything.

Jesus Calling affirms, "LIVING IN DEPENDENCE ON ME is a glorious adventure … You begin each day with joyful expectation, watching to see what I will do. You accept weakness as a gift from Me, knowing that *My Power plugs in most readily to consecrated weakness.* You keep your plans tentative, knowing that My plans are far superior. *You consciously live, move, and have your being in Me,* desiring that I live in you. I in you, and you in Me. This is the intimate adventure I offer you."[100]

Philippians 4:11–13 declares, "I have learned to be content whatever the circumstances. I know what it is to be in need, and I know what it is to have plenty. I have learned the secret of being content in any and every situation, whether well fed or hungry, whether living in plenty or in want. I can do everything through him who gives me strength." Paul was completely about spreading the Gospel and glorifying God. He proclaimed, "I have been crucified with Christ and I no longer live, but Christ lives in me. The life I live in the body, I live by faith in the Son of God, who loved me and gave himself for me" (Galatians 2:20). He could do everything God asked him to do, because Christ was his and he was Christ's.

Read Romans 8:12–17.

"For you did not receive a spirit that makes you a slave again to fear, but you received the Spirit of sonship … The Spirit himself testifies with our spirit that we are God's children … heirs of God and co-heirs of Christ, if indeed we share in his sufferings in order that we may also share in his glory" (Romans 8:15–17).

We are God's beloved children. Our Prince Charming has reached His hand out to us. He does offer us "happily ever after," and while it may not be in this earthly life, He offers us His grace and His power, and that's all we'll need here. He has given us His all. Will we give Him our all? Can we say the following prayer and mean it? If not, then ask God to help you grow into it.

A COVENANT PRAYER

I am no longer my own but Thine.
Put me to what Thou wilt.
Rank me with whom Thou wilt.
Put me to doing, put me to suffering.
Let me be employed for Thee or laid aside for Thee,
Exalted for Thee or brought low for Thee.
Let me be full, let me be empty.

---

[100] Young, Sarah. *Jesus Calling*, p. 257. September 2.

Let me have all things, let me have nothing.
I freely and earnestly yield all things to Thy pleasure and disposal.
And now, Glorious and Blessed God,
Father, Son, and Holy Spirit,
Thou art mine, and I am Thine.
So be it.
And the covenant which I have made on earth,
Let it be ratified in heaven.
Amen.[101]

How is God using this lesson to equip you? Record meaningful statements, ideas, and scriptures you may want to remember and use as He equips you for the task for which He is calling you.

_____

_____

_____

_____

_____

_____

_____

---

[101] A Covenant Prayer in the Wesleyan Tradition — as used in the *Book of Offices of the British Methodist Church*, 1936.

Day 5

PAUL'S RECIPES: "ANXIETY-FREE RECIPE" AND "CULTIVATING THE ATTITUDE"

CHEF PAUL SHARES HIS SECRET RECIPES

*I*F YOU'VE EVER BEEN ON car duty that first week of school, you might have seen this phenomenon: The first day, just about everyone comes bounding off the bus or out of cars dressed in their trendy back-to-school outfits, bearing backpacks stuffed with brand new school supplies. Later that same week, the principal is out there with you amidst the crying and whining. He is getting ready to peel the "fit-pitcher" out of the car, but he pleads one more time, "Please, Mrs. Lester, your class is waiting on you."

It's all about attitude. Charles Swindoll, the prolific writer and pastor, has some great thoughts on attitude: "The longer I live, the more I realize the impact of attitude on life. Attitude, to me, is more important than facts. It is more important than the past, than education, than money, than circumstances, than failures, than successes, than what other people think or say or do. It is more important than appearance, giftedness or skill. It will make or break a company … [a school] … a church … a home. The remarkable thing is we have a choice every day regarding the attitude we will embrace for that day. We cannot change our past … we cannot change the fact that people will act in a certain way. We cannot change the inevitable. The only thing we can do is play on the one string we have, and that is our attitude … I am convinced that life is 10% what happens to me and 90% how I react to it. And so it is with you … we are in charge of our attitudes."[102]

We are bombarded on a daily basis by positive and negative stimuli: people, objects, events, ideas, activities, situations, etc. Our evaluations of all those stimuli based on our nature and our experiences evokes a response—our attitude.

- Would you say you are generally an optimist, a pessimist, or a cynic (a frustrated optimist)?

  _____

  _____

  _____

  _____

---

[102] Swindoll, Charles. http://www.bigeye.com/attitude.htm.

- Do you agree with Swindoll that life is 10 percent what happens to you and 90 percent your reaction?

_____

_____

_____

_____

Medical scientists believe that depression and varying degrees of mental illness are the result of "perceived absence of control over the outcome of a situation,"[103] and there are a plethora of reasons teachers are feeling frustration in their ability to make a difference in schools today. Perhaps this is what Mrs. Lester was feeling as summer vacation masked the anxiety that hatched into reality and rear-ended her in the first week of school.

Paul knew these feelings also. In his ministry, there were plenty of situations over which he had no control. The important difference was that he knew the One who did have control, and Paul gave Him full sway. Early in his ministry, in his first letter to the Thessalonians, Paul was working on his recipe for dealing with anxiety. He admonished them to "always try to be kind to each other and to everyone else. Be joyful always; pray continually; give thanks in all circumstances, for this is God's will for you in Christ Jesus" (1 Thessalonians 5:15–18). But in Philippians, Paul perfected his recipe.

- _Read Philippians 4:4–7_ and write down the steps in "Paul's Anxiety-free Recipe."

_____

_____

_____

_____

The first ingredient is _rejoice in the Lord always_. He even gave it a second measure of REJOICE. While it's probably the very last thing we _feel_ like doing when our attitude is ailing, it's a call out of ourselves and away from ourselves to the One who loves us and will work with us in all the situations that cause us anxiety. Paul is not saying we should be happy—happiness is a surface feeling. Joy is deep and rich, a taproot which connects us to our Father God.

What is the first thing a toddler does when he gets hurt or gets into a jam? The toddler looks up for his mother or father, for he knows he is loved and is watched over, and his parent is close. It is the same with our Father God. The longer we toddle around with God, the more we can rely on Him and our rejoicing comes quicker. We rejoice that He loves us, that we are watched over, and that He is close. Paul even says, "The Lord is near" in verse 5. We know

---

[103] Seligman, M. E. P. (1975). _Helplessness: On Depression, Development, and Death_. San Francisco: W. H. Freeman. ISBN 0-7167-2328-X. http://en.wikipedia.org/wiki/Learned_helplessness.

everything will be OK with our Heavenly Father near to us. That's good reason for that second measure of REJOICE!

The next step is to *be gentle*. As Christians, we are called to love others, and that's not easy at times. In Philippians 4:2, Paul was pleading with Euodia and Synthyche, both coworkers of his, to quit quarrelling and be friends again. Being gentle with each other, being considerate and unselfish was a starting place in their reconciliation. It's hard to act lovingly toward the youngster in your class who has just exploded verbally and physically toward his classmates. The children probably won't remember what you said to rectify the situation, but they will remember your gentleness in dealing with them.

The third ingredient is *prayer* with a cupful of *petition* or supplication and several scoops of *thanksgiving*. In essence, Paul was saying, "Child, run to your Father with your concerns. Tell Him what happened and what upset you. Ask Him humbly and earnestly to help you fix it and heal it. Stop and *listen* to Him. Give Him a big hug, and tell Him what an amazing Father He is. Let Him know how glad you are that you are His child and how grateful you are for everything He has done for you. Then run off and do the next thing you are called to do in gentleness and with rejoicing."

If we follow the recipe, Paul says, it will produce a peace and wholeness and depth of joy that far exceeds our expectations of protection and security. In fact, he says, our hearts and minds will be "guarded in Christ Jesus." We are, as Colossians 3:3 says, "hidden with Christ in God," so whatever it is that is causing our anxiety will have to contend with God before it gets to us. Now that's some kind of comfort.

In the next two verses of Philippians, Paul whips up another secret recipe. This one is for "cultivating and strengthening a Christian attitude."

* *Read Philippians 4:8–9*, and list the things on which Paul says we should focus.

_____

_____

_____

_____

At first glance, Paul's advice seems simplistic and out of touch, but is it not we who are out of touch? Have we become so indoctrinated to the "noise" and protocol of the worldly that Paul's thinking seems prudish and strange?

For instance, Paul counsels us to think about what is true. Now that's a tricky one in today's political climate. A person can get dizzy from all the spin. If some incident happened in front of five individuals, there would probably be five different versions of truth. We can't depend on public opinion; we can't depend on media, government, industry, or even religion to tell us the truth. Our true north is God—we can only orient ourselves in Him and His Word. The most basic truth is God is love. He loved us so much He gave His own Son for us (John 3:16). Only in spending time with God can His Holy Spirit help us discern truth.

Paul instructs us to think about what right. His kind of right isn't the "Well, everybody is doing it" kind of right. His is the kind of right that we just can't ignore, that costs us a little more time and trouble but is the right and honorable and even noble thing to do. The world's "right" manifests itself in temptation to cut corners, take shortcuts, or bend the rules regarding truth, accuracy, timing, courtesy, or even decency—"the end justifies the means" kind of thinking. Paul's "right" is not glorification of self but unequivocal glorification of God.

For the most part, pure, lovely, and admirable seem out of our reach. What is the world's excellent or praiseworthy anyway? Is it celebrity? The world tells us we're not enough. We're not pretty or handsome enough, skinny enough, smart enough, stylish enough, good enough for anyone to admire us. Sadly, in our longing to be outstanding, infamy is almost as desirable as celebrity today.

Honestly, it's hard to even recognize good sometimes because this world has deceived us so. Is "good" getting together to pray for others if it becomes a "glorified" excuse to gossip? Is it good and conscientious to stay late at school to be prepared for the students the next day? Or is it a "lofty" justification for being obsessive, a workaholic, and cheating those who love you out of time spent with you? How bent does "good" have to be before it arcs into something that is not?

Sarah Young, in *Jesus Calling*, says, "There is a mighty battle going on for control of your mind … The world exerts a downward pull on your thoughts."[104] She says greed and lust and cynicism are rampant. Paul wrote in Romans 8:6, "The mind of sinful man is death, but the mind controlled by the Spirit is life and peace." Paul calls us to focus—focus on good and positive things. He told the Philippians to focus on what he taught them when he was there with them— on what they heard him say and saw him do. If there had been bibles around back then, Paul would have been telling them to dig in and see what Jesus said and did.

Paul's recipe may call for some substitutions in our lives. Instead of hard rock or country music, we could try the Christian music channel. There's absolutely nothing wrong with rock or country, but the praise music might lift our spirits. Could there be less rage on the road when we're singing to the Lord?

There are choices in the books we read, the television programs and movies we watch, the way we spend our time and money. In Romans 12:2, Paul advises, "Do not conform any longer to the pattern of this world, but be transformed by the renewing of your mind. Then you will be able to test and approve what God's will is—his good, pleasing and perfect will." This is what Paul was after.

There are many things in this world over which we have no control, but we don't have to let the world control us. We can, in fact, have our minds renewed as we make choices to focus on good things. Just as Charles Swindoll said, "We are in charge of our attitudes." We can see tough circumstances as opportunities, just as Paul did. We can remain at peace in stormy seas, as Paul did. The more we strengthen our Christian attitude muscles, the more the "God of peace" will be with us.

---

[104] Young, Sarah. *Jesus Calling*, p. 274. September 19.

Finally, remember that attitude and feelings aren't the same; they do not go hand and hand. Attitude should not be held hostage by emotions. The only emotions Paul elicits are thankfulness and rejoicing. All other negative emotions, when it is all said and done, is lack of faith in the One who is in control. Keep your negative feelings out of the kitchen, and Paul's recipes will yield peace in this uncertain world. Bon appétit.

How is God using this lesson to equip you? Record meaningful statements, ideas, and scriptures you may want to remember and use as He equips you for the task for which He is calling you.

GROUP QUESTIONS FOR PAUL WAS CALLED

- Explain and discuss the three kinds of grace: prevenient (preparing) grace, justifying (accepting) grace, and sanctifying (sustaining) grace.

- What does it mean to be "broken bread and poured out wine" for others? In your family? At school? At church?

- What is the difference between being "broken bread and poured out wine" for others and fostering codependency or being a workaholic?

- When you consider that a chain is only as strong as its weakest link, what can be done to strengthen and bring unity to a body of workers? How might gifts of the Spirit and fruits of the Spirit come into play?

- Discuss the ironies of living a "fairy tale life" and trying to control your "happily ever after" in light of being a child of God.

- *God Calling* says, "Praise is the devil's death knell." Motivational speaker Zig Ziglar coined the phrase "Have an attitude of gratitude." Consider how these quotes speak to Paul's instructions, "Rejoice in the Lord always" (Philippians 4:4). What are some concrete ways these ideas can be put into practice?

You Are Called

WEEK 6

Day 1

REPENT—EMPTY YOUR HANDS AND TAKE HOLD OF GOD

CHALKBOARD SURVIVOR OR CHALKBOARD THRIVER?

Dear Ann Landers: I'm sure your readers have seen the reality TV shows that are currently popular. Most of them involve some sort of physical and mental challenge. I have a game for them.

Drop three businessmen and three businesswomen into an elementary school classroom for six weeks. Each contestant will be provided with a class of 28 students and a copy of the school district's curriculum. Each class will have five learning-disabled children, three with Attention Deficit Disorder, one gifted child, two who speak limited English and three labeled as having severe behavioral problems.

Each contestant must complete lesson plans at least three days in advance with curriculum objectives, and modify, organize and create materials to match. They will be required to teach students, handle misconduct, implement technology, document attendance, write referrals, correct homework, make bulletin boards, compute grades, complete report cards, communicate with parents and arrange conferences. They must also supervise recess and monitor the hallways, and complete drills in case of fires, tornadoes, or shooting attacks. They must attend workshops, faculty meetings, union meetings and curriculum development meetings.

If they are sick or having a bad day, they must not let it show. They must maintain discipline and provide an educationally stimulating environment. They can golf on the weekends, but on their new salary, they won't be able to afford it.

The winner of the contest will be allowed to return to his or her job.

—Teaching Is Not Easy, Harrisburg, Pa.

Dear Harrisburg: I doubt any TV producers will go for your idea, but I'm sure every teacher in my reading audience will appreciate your version of reality. Teaching may not be easy, but a good teacher is worth his or her weight in gold.

—Austin American Statesman, Saturday, March 9, 2002

$\mathcal{T}$HE LETTER TO ANN LANDERS was written years ago, and things have gotten even harder and more complicated since then. Teaching or having a job in which you deal with the public or with people in your workplace is not easy; in fact, sometimes it's downright ridiculous. For example, a teacher with twenty-two students has to deal with as many as forty-four parents, and the number of involved adults goes up exponentially with stepparents. Junior high and high school teachers multiply that by the number of classes they teach. Do you have days when you feel like you are drowning in your job? You fight and fight to keep your head above water, but you're tired, and you don't seem to be getting anywhere? You see no rescue, no relief in sight?

Moses felt like that. He was surrounded and drowning in complaints of the Israelites. David was dodging spears and running for his life. Queen Esther contemplated facing death if she did something and sure death if she did nothing. Paul was shipwrecked, beaten, starved, stoned—just another day in paradise.

Ridiculous circumstances, ridiculously difficult people to deal with—but each one of these Bible characters had a ridiculous-to-the-world faith that God would lead and equip them. If you are still reading this after five weeks of this study, *you are called*, and if you truly believe God is calling you—even in YOUR circumstances—then you too can believe that *you will be equipped.*

We're not talking about being equipped merely to escape our circumstances/problems, nor are we talking about summoning God to zap us into superhero suits, imploring Him follow us as we wade into the difficult places according to *our* plan. No. The first step is to do something the world reviles: Stop. The prince of this world wants to keep us fearful and frantic and running, so he keeps whispering worldly theology in our ears: Don't stop! Keep going, or you'll never be a success. Don't be a wimp—you're supposed to be self-sufficient!

We are like adventurous toddlers exploring the world. Sometimes we get so caught up in the world and its distractions, we don't even realize we have wandered away from our Father. We experience stumbles, falls, bumps, bruises, and still we wander—and then we *wonder* how we got so lost.

Psalm 46:10 says, "Be still, and know that I am God." Be still, and *read Psalm 46:1–3.*

"Therefore we will not fear, though the earth give way and the mountains fall into the heart of the sea" (Psalm 46:2). Can you imagine this scene: a mountain drops into the sea before us and we're not to be afraid? Scripture reveals if our world collapses around us, God is "an ever present help in trouble."

Repent is the end of wandering. It means to *stop*, turn around, and go the other direction. Repenting is not a passive, mumbled confession like children who apologize for something and go right back to the same behavior. It is the active realization that we've been going the wrong way, going our own path—away from God and His ways. When we truly repent, we turn back to God and seek to follow His path.

There are two church seasons of the year that speak in depth about repent: Advent and Lent. In Advent, we hear Isaiah's words about John the Baptist: "The voice of him that crieth in the wilderness, 'Prepare ye the way of the Lord, make straight in the desert a highway for our God. Every valley shall be exalted, and every mountain and hill shall be made low; and the crooked shall be made straight, and rough places plain. And the glory of the Lord shall be revealed, and all flesh shall see it together; for the mouth of the Lord hath spoken it'"[105] (Isaiah 40:3–5).

Do you see a similarity in the readings from Psalm 46 and Isaiah 40? Upheaval. In his commentary, Matthew Henry[106] believed Isaiah meant the dejected and despondent would be "raised up" and "those that are hindered from comfort in Christ by a proud conceit of their own merit and worth are the mountains and hills that must be made low." The "crooked" are those with "corrupt inclinations." All will experience upheaval so their need for the Lord will be revealed to them.

Sometimes we humans don't get God's subtle attempts to get our attention. We keep going our own direction until there is significant turmoil in our lives. Often it takes a 2x4 of anxiety, illness, hardship, stress, and loss before we realize the need to turn and return to God.

Another way to look at repentance is this: "When you're full of yourself, God can't fill you. But when you empty yourself, God has a useful vessel."[107] During the Lenten season, this question is often asked: What is it that is coming between you and a deeper relationship with God? What would that be for you at this time in your life?

_____

_____

_____

_____

Whatever your answer is, ask God to help you see how that separation can be resolved.

Repenting isn't a one-time deal. Repenting, turning to God, recognizing our need for Christ, prepares our hearts to truly receive Him. It is the attitude that we don't know the whole picture, but we know that "the eyes of the Lord range throughout the earth to strengthen those whose hearts are fully committed to Him" (2 Chronicles 16:9). We are not in control, but we know the One who is, and we come. Repenting—continually and intentionally turning to Christ—paves the way to come and receive from Him. It was that way in the time of John the Baptist, and it is that way still.

- In your experience and thinking, what are the qualities of a good student?

_____

_____

_____

_____

---

[105] Isaiah 40:3–5, King James Version.
[106] Henry, Matthew. *Matthew Henry's Commentary*, vol. 4, p. 213.
[107] Lucado, Max. *Cure for the Common Life*, p. 88.

- Using your responses of the qualities of a good student, reverse it, and ask yourself if you are a good student of the Master Teacher according to your own expectations.

_____

_____

_____

_____

There are many qualities of a good disciple (student), but in a word, students must be receptive. Disciples must turn to their teacher and be present and attentive. They must make time to do their homework—reading scripture, practicing scriptural truths in daily life, praying and calling on God, and even being alert to life's "pop quizzes." The Master Teacher personalizes our assignments. Heed Him.

Jesus knew firsthand that life is hard. He knew after He was gone, it would only get harder, so He prayed for you. *Read John 17:6–23.*

God wants us to be in the world but not of the world. "You are the salt of the earth. But if the salt loses its saltiness, how can it be made salty again?" (Matthew 5:13) M. Robert Mulholland, Jr.[108] spoke of the world's outrageous need for equipped men and women:

> A world characterized by deep valleys of despair and hopelessness desperately needs the witness of a community filled with the unquenchable assurance that comes from a life "hid with Christ in God" (Colossians 3:3). A world distinguished by mountains of violence and injustice urgently needs the presence of a community whose humble life of other-referenced Love stands sacrificially against entrenched structures of injustice. A world misshapen by the crookedness of the false values of a pervasively self-referenced way of being crucially needs the example of a radically different way of being, that of a community whose values enhance and enrich human life and wholeness. A world diseased with the roughness of intolerance and prejudice critically needs the model of a community in which all are welcomed in the healing love of God and nurtured to wholeness in the image of God.

Life is just flat messy. *Jesus Calling* says, "I challenge you to relinquish the fantasy of an uncluttered world. Accept each day just as it comes, and find Me in the midst of it all." We are admonished not to let our to-do lists become idols directing our lives, that "a successful day is one in which you have stayed in touch with Me, even if many things remain undone at the end of the day."[109]

---

[108] Mulholland, M. Robert, Jr. *Preparing the Way of the Lord*, p. 356. Disciplines 2012. Upper Room Books.
[109] Young, Sarah. *Jesus Calling*, p. 96.

Yes, you are called, and you will be equipped. Will you be a chalkboard survivor or a chalkboard thriver?

How is God using this lesson to equip you? Record meaningful statements, ideas, and scriptures you may want to remember and use as He equips you for the task for which He is calling you.

_____

_____

_____

_____

_____

_____

Day 2

BEING PRESENT TO GOD

IS THE HOKEY POKEY REALLY WHAT IT'S ALL ABOUT?

"*Y*OU PUT YOUR RIGHT HAND in. You take your right hand out. You put your right hand in and you shake it all about. You do the hokey pokey and you turn yourself around. That's what it's all about." Then you put in your left hand, right foot, left foot, right hip, left hip, and even your head. You turn and spin and shake and clap, and after you've done all of this, you've pretty well figured out that you have no idea "what it's all about!"

The world will tell you this makeup, that diet, this exercise program, that outfit will make you happy. It tells you that principal, this school, that program, this group of kids, that curriculum will make you successful. This vacation, that church, this neighborhood, that group of friends will fulfill you. The world focuses on the outside, on things external, and how these things influence and affect you. We bounce around through life like a pinball pinging off these external stimuli, but inside, we know this is not "what it's all about."

Read Mark 15:33–39.

As Jesus hung on the cross, the earth was enveloped in darkness, symbolic of the sin of the world that collided with the Son of God that day and, indeed, seemed victorious. As Jesus breathed His last breath, three of the Gospels report that "the curtain of the temple was torn in two," from top to bottom. How many times have we read that line with a modicum of curiosity and hurried past it toward resurrection? Even before the resurrection of Christ, immediately upon His death, an earth-shattering thing took place—God tore open the curtain that separated Him from us.

Back in the Exodus days of Moses, God gave specific directives concerning the construction of a tabernacle, a sanctuary, so that God could "dwell among" His people. The Most Holy Place or Holy of Holies was the inner room where God's presence abided, shielded from sinful man by a thick veil or curtain. One day a year the Israelites observed a high holy day, the Day of Atonement, in which the high priest, properly cleansed and prepared, would enter the Holy of Holies and sprinkle the blood of sacrifice for his sins and the sins of the people (Hebrews 9:7).

Centuries later, before Jesus's ministry began, "John the baptizer saw Jesus coming toward him and said, 'Look, the Lamb of God, who takes away the sin of the world!'" (John 1:29) That prophesy came true. While God's heart was broken at the suffering of His Son, the moment Jesus died, the thick curtain that shielded God from sinful man was torn in two. The Lamb of God had been slain, sacrificed for our sin, and the blood of the Lamb atoned for our sins once and for all. We are "at one" with God, cleansed and "right" before Him.

Jesus paid for our entrance into the Holy of Holies with His life, and God tore back the curtains and welcomed us into His presence and into His heart. *Read* how the apostle Paul interprets it in *Hebrews 10:19–23*.

The world is consumed by external things, but internally, we are left empty. God in Christ welcomes us into His presence, and in the depth of our being, we find peace and unconditional love. In 2 Corinthians 4:18, it says, "Things that are visible are brief and fleeting, while things that are invisible are deathless and everlasting."[110] The piece of our heart that was missing is found in the peace and presence of God. We don't have to depend on a priest or any other intermediary to go to God on our behalf. Amazingly enough, the God of the universe wants a profound relationship with us!

Now it's up to us. It's our choice to pursue this relationship, for we can't sit on the fence. *Read* what Christ says about fence-sitters in *Revelation 3:14–22*.

Can't you just see the proud Laodiceans receiving this message? Isn't it rich that Christ says these smart, prosperous, self-sufficient people are to be pitied? It's reminiscent of the story of the emperor's clothes. Christ is knocking, wanting to be with them, and they're smugly standing there in their birthday suits! *Jesus Calling* declares, "Each moment you can choose to practice My Presence or to practice the presence of problems."[111] What have you chosen?

- How do you experience the presence of God? At home? At school?

_____

_____

_____

Long before Facebook, Twitter, and smartphones were around—even before Internet, TV, and radio—lived a quiet, unassuming, and simple man named Nicholas Herman. As a soldier during the Thirty Years War, he suffered a crippling injury resulting in disability and lifelong pain. He spent time as a civil servant, but finally, in middle age, he entered a Paris monastery and worked in the kitchen. While not having acquired the education to study for the priesthood, many were drawn to his deep-rooted serenity and would come to him for spiritual guidance. Brother Lawrence, as he was called, spoke volumes by his actions and demeanor, but it wasn't until after his death that his "technique" became available, as a result of personal interviews and letters, in a booklet titled *The Practice of the Presence of God*.

His technique began with faith—that God is God and we are not, so instead of pursuing our own way, we should pursue His way. By conversing with God, keeping Him continually at the forefront of our thoughts and actions during the day, we will be in God's presence and will be doing His will. "You would think it rude to leave a friend alone who came to visit you. Why, then, must God be neglected?"[112] Why, he would reason, would we dare to "busy ourselves with trifles which do not please Him and perhaps even offend Him?"

---

[110] The Amplified Bible.
[111] Young, Sarah. *Jesus Calling*, p. 104. April 9.
[112] *The Practice of the Presence of God*.

Brother Lawrence admitted that this practice didn't come easily; in fact, it took ten years before his flagging devotion and heightened unworthiness were quenched by inner peace. He reportedly prayed this prayer before he started his workday:

> O my God, since Thou art with me, and I must now, in obedience to Thy commands, apply my mind to these outward things, I beseech Thee to grant me the grace to continue in Thy Presence; and to this end do Thou prosper me with Thy assistance. Receive all my works, and possess all my affections.

He was said to have detested kitchen work, but "having accustomed himself to do everything there for the love of God and asking for God's grace to do his work well, he had found everything easy during the fifteen years that he had been employed there."

Having taught for many years, the teacher noticed how many untied shoelaces she would see in a day, not just in kindergarten but in first, second, and third grade as well. "Don't parents teach their kids how to tie their shoes anymore? They should at least buy shoes with Velcro ties," she reasoned. Then she heard, "'Let the little children come unto me.' Aren't you here to serve?" Although it wasn't as easy to get down on her knees as it used to be, she did and called to the straggle-laced kid. As she started to tie, she noticed the shoelaces were wet with no puddles anywhere in sight. She sighed and thought, *This one's for You, Lord*, and she smiled and prayed for the little boy by name. Before she could get up, another youngster pulled up for a tie, and she prayed for that student by name. On her knees, she tied four pairs of shoes and prayed for four students and their families. Subsequently, instead of an irritation, an untied shoelace became an opportunity to practice the presence of God.

- Can you think of unpleasant classroom tasks that could become opportunities to practice the presence of God?

  _____

  _____

  _____

- Are you on the watch for blessings throughout the day, and do you readily offer thanks?

  _____

  _____

  _____

- Do you often ask God to assist you during the day with tasks that are for His supreme glory?

  _____

  _____

  _____

- What is your ultimate purpose for your day—is it to simply get through the day, or is it to glorify God?

_____

_____

_____

Jesus Calling says, "Learn to live above your circumstances. This requires focused time with Me, the *One who overcame the world.* Trouble and distress are woven into the very fabric of this perishing world. Only My Life in you can empower you to face this endless flow of problems with *good cheer.* As you sit quietly in My Presence, I shine Peace into your troubled mind and heart. Little by little, you are freed from earthly shackles and lifted up above your circumstances. You gain My perspective on your life, enabling you to distinguish between what is important and what is not. Rest in My Presence, *receiving Joy that no one can take away from you.*"[113]

"You put your whole self in. You take your whole self out. You put your whole self in and you shake it all about. You do the hokey pokey and you turn yourself around. That's what it's all about." It's not hocus-pocus, and it's not the hokey pokey. Being wholly present to God—*that's* what it's all about!

Whatever you do, do it all for the glory of God.
—1 Corinthians 10:31

Rewrite Brother Lawrence's prayer before work in your own words:

_____

_____

_____

_____

_____

_____

_____

---

[113] Young, Sarah. *Jesus Calling*, p. 76. March 13.

Day 3
THY ROD AND STAFF DEVELOPMENT PLAN

DR. BENJAMIN SPOCK, MEET PROFESSOR PROVERB

ONE WORD OF ADVICE MOST teachers would share with young parents is that children need boundaries, for limitations lovingly enforced provide security for a child. Youngsters need time to explore and grow in a safe environment on which they can count, even if they don't always understand the reasoning behind the limitations.

Conversely, children who are not given boundaries will push until parents, teachers, or even law enforcement finally do set them. They experience more anxiety and outbursts because they are not secure and cannot understand the negative impact some decisions ultimately have despite the immediate positive results they experienced at the time.

Today's children are well-versed in their rights, while many of us, who remember archaic things like party lines and brush hair rollers, didn't have rights as children and don't seem to have them now.

Proverbs has a lot to say about creating boundaries for children:

> 3:11–12: "My son, do not despise the LORD's discipline
> and do not resent his rebuke,
> Because the LORD disciplines those he loves,
> as a father the son he delights in."

> 13:24: "He who spares the rod hates his son,
> but he who loves him is careful to discipline him."

> 22:6: "Train a child in the way he should go,
> and when he is old he will not turn from it."

> 22:15: "Foolishness is bound up in the heart of a child,
> but the rod of discipline will drive it far from him."

> 29:15: "The rod of correction imparts wisdom,
> but a child left to itself disgraces his mother."

Did you hear anything about rights? No, but there is much about the rod. Back in biblical days, the rod was something that you didn't leave home without. It was a wooden staff, either straight or with a crook, that was used as a walking stick, a defense mechanism or weapon, a shepherd's tool, a measuring stick, a symbol of authority, and even as a tool to thresh grain.[114] Other resources speak of the rod separate from the shepherd's staff,[115] but predominately, they are used for support and setting boundaries, keeping threats away and guiding toward good things.

Read how the rod and staff are used in *Psalm 23*.

This is absolutely *not* a treatise on corporeal punishment, and it certainly is not a judgment piece about child-rearing. The rod most certainly has been used to "beat" some sense into others, but this is not the way it is used by the Shepherd in Psalm 23, and we, in authority of our classrooms and our homes, must lovingly shepherd our flock as the Shepherd in Psalm 23 did: We must know and value each one of our charges. Are they tired or overstimulated? Do they feel bullied? Do they need some space? Do they need to be challenged? We must skillfully and gingerly carry our rods of discipline to provide boundaries that are consistent and comforting, for some of our children are walking through valleys and scary places. We anoint our students with encouragement and provide a risk-free learning environment. Hopefully, however, they will not dwell in our classrooms forever!

- Have you been a good shepherd for your children?
- How does Psalm 23 make you feel in your ovine journey (as a sheep)?

_____

_____

_____

- Refer to Proverbs 3:11-12. When the Lord has His rod after us prodding us to go one way and we want to go another, do we "resent his rebuke," or can we recognize His love and care and cede to His will?

We probably don't always recognize that many times our circumstances are a "squeeze" play by a loving and protective Father who is reaching out with His rod to guide us. We are caught between a tantrum and boundaries lovingly enforced, but if we can stop and look up to our Father as we ponder life's questions and predicaments, perhaps we will see those "paths of righteousness."

It is especially true as we try to shepherd our students. Twenty-two lives with all the experiences and people they bring into the mix of your flock is daunting. How can we do this? Have a visit with the Good Shepherd, the Master Teacher, on the following pages.

---

[114] *The Revell Bible Dictionary*, p. 870.
[115] Keller, Phillip. Excerpts from: *A Shepherd Looks at Psalm 23*. http://www.antipas.org/commentaries/articles/shepherd_psa23/shepherd_07.

THY ROD AND THY STAFF DEVELOPMENT PLAN*

Plan before the school year begins or at the beginning of every semester: Meditate on these questions before God and see His direction for the school year.

- Do you think you were "called" to teach? What gifts do you bring to teaching? What are you thankful for in this job? How has teaching blessed you?
- What are the hardest times of the school year for you? What about this time of the school year can you change? How can you change your attitude toward this challenging time?
- What situations at school leave you feeling grumpy, frustrated, anxious, fearful, defensive, or hopeless? What about the situation can you change? How does God want to use the parts of the situation you cannot change?
- Are there colleagues or people on staff who are difficult with whom to work? Any parents with whom it is hard to deal? Is God working through these people? Is God able to use you in this situation, or is your pride and your sense of righteousness in the way?
- Are there children with whom you dread dealing? Is the problem their temperament or their environment or both? How would Jesus tell you to deal with them?
- Can you get a prayer partner for the things and people you can't change, the situations which cause you the most stress?
- Many times criticism is not about us, but it's the "last straw" in another person's life. Can you keep from getting defensive or letting it spoil your joy? If the criticism is warranted, however, can you graciously accept it?
- Do you have a plan for spiritual study this year to exercise your spiritual health? Do you have a scripture theme for this school year?
- Do you have a plan for physical exercise this year for bodily health and to help de-stress?
- Are you serving God with your whole heart in school, or is it just a job? Give God your school year, and try to be present to His direction. Let Him be your co-teacher. He wants to be in your school.
- Will you tithe 10 percent of your planning time to reflect with God at the end of the school day?

*Psalm 23: "Thy rod and thy staff they comfort me."

Daily Rod and Staff Development Plan

[Your 10 Percent Tithe of Planning Time]

- Take some deep breaths and relax your shoulders.

- Ask God to join you as you reflect on the day and to guide your thoughts as you seek His will for you.

- Did you feel God's presence in your classroom today? How?

- What happened during this day for which you are thankful?

- Are there any red flags (fear, anger, anxiety, stress, feeling trapped, hopelessness, guilt, frustration) that you need to bring before God? Your Father was there— what is His perspective on it?

- Is there one overriding concern today? Put your concern into perspective. In the total picture, how important is it? How is God telling you to handle it?

- Did you let someone spoil your joy today? If criticism was unwarranted, did you pray a silent prayer for them? If it was warranted, did you receive it graciously?

- Did you "let your gentleness be evident to all"?*

- Ask God to bless the rest of your planning time—that it would be accurate for the children's needs and efficient for your needs and that you would be calm, focused, relaxed as you finish your day.

- Amen!

* Philippians 4:4–9: "Rejoice in the Lord always. I will say it again: Rejoice! *Let your gentleness be evident to all.* The Lord is near. Do not be anxious about anything, but in everything, by prayer and petition, with thanksgiving, present your requests to God. And the peace of God, which transcends all understanding, will guard your hearts and your minds in Christ Jesus. Finally, brothers, whatever is true, whatever is noble, whatever is right, whatever is pure, whatever is lovely, whatever is admirable—if anything is excellent or praiseworthy—think about such things. Whatever you have learned or received or heard from me, or seen in me—put into practice. And the God of peace will be with you."

Day 4

FOCUSED RELATIONSHIP WITH CHRIST AFFECTS ALL RELATIONSHIPS

KEEPING THE MAIN THING THE MAIN THING.

FROM COVER TO COVER, THE Bible is about relationships—relationship with God and relationships with one another. We have walked with five individuals who were in relationship with God. We saw how God called them, and we learned how He equipped each one of them to fulfill His call. Moses, David, Esther, Jesus, and Paul were all called to shepherd God's people.

Teaching is a premier shepherding gig. Often the nine-month journey with a flock is grueling, and sheep sure aren't what they used to be. In days past, if you could get one sheep headed in the right direction, they would all follow; they really didn't want to stand out from the fold. But with today's lambs, it's totally different—not the homogenous flock of yesteryear. Various ethnicities, customs, religions, talents, abilities, opportunities or lack thereof, and varying stages of readiness to learn make the job very challenging for their teacher-shepherd. In addition, modern education has, unfortunately, done its best to remove student-teacher relationships in favor of standardized, cookie-cutter education. The only thing the public ever hears about student-teacher relationships is when they are inappropriate. Most students today don't come intrinsically motivated, and finding extrinsic incentives that work in our "let's give everybody a trophy" society is more than a challenge for our teacher-shepherds.

When we've hit the wall of vocational frustration, Max Lucado, in his book *Cure for the Common Life*, offers this thought: "We have two bosses: one who signs our checks and one who saves our souls. The second has keen interest in our workaday world. What if everyone worked with God in mind? Suppose no one worked to satisfy self or please the bottom line but everyone worked to please God."[116]

- Think about it. What would that look like in your school? In your classroom?

_____

_____

_____

---

[116] Lucado, Max. *Cure for the Common Life*, p. 94.

- *Read Ephesians 6:7,* and write it down.

_____

_____

_____

- *Read 1 Corinthians 10:31b,* and finish the quote: "Whatever …

_____

_____

_____

Do you remember the Prozac-inducing passage in the Ecclesiastes reading in Day 1 of Moses? "All is vanity. What do people gain from all the toil?" (Ecclesiastes 1:2, 3) Our work *is* "vanity" if it is done in and of ourselves, but if it is done in the spirit of 1 Corinthians 10:31, then it is kingdom-building and God-empowered—anything but vanity!

Lucado wrote,

> I have a friend who understands this. By job description she teaches at a public elementary school. By God's description she pastors a class of precious children. Read the e-mail she sent her friends:
>
> > I'm asking for your prayers for my students. I know everyone is busy, but if you ever can, I know there is power in specifically addressed prayers. Please pray for …
> >
> > Randy (smartest boy in my class—mom speaks no English—just moved from Washington—blind in his right eye because he poked his eye with a sharp tool when he was three)
> >
> > Henry (learning disabled—tries with all his little heart—it takes him about a minute to say two words—I think he's used to me now, but it was hard for him to keep up at first!)
> >
> > Richard (a smile that could almost get him out of any trouble—his mom can't be much older than I am—he's very smart and pretty naughty, just the way I like 'em!)
> >
> > Anna (learning disability—neither parent can read, write, or drive—they have four children!!! Who knows how they keep it together—colors me a picture every single day, writes her spelling sentences about me, I'm the main character in her stories.)
> >
> > On and on the list goes, including nearly deaf Sara. Disorganized-but-thoughtful Terrell. Model-student Alicia. Bossy-but-creative Kaelyn.
>
> Does this teacher work for a school system or for God? Does she spend her day in work or worship? Does she make money or a difference?[117]

---

[117] Ibid., pp. 98–99.

Doesn't that just take your breath away? That's relationship—first with the Father, His Son, and His Holy Spirit; and then with students, parents, families, fellow teachers, staff, and friends and family outside of school. Are those students in the presence of God every day? You bet they are. Does that teacher practice the presence of God? Absolutely.

Does that teacher ever have a tough day? Sure she does, but she knows it's not all up to her. When things don't go as planned, she can take a deep breath and ask God to show her what to do. *Jesus Calling* says to "remember that I am sovereign over your circumstances, and humble yourself under My mighty hand. Rejoice in what I am doing in your life, even though it is beyond your understanding."[118] "I am not a careless God. When I allow difficulties to come into your life, I equip you fully to handle them. Relax in My Presence, trusting in My Strength." "God grants us an uncommon life to the degree we surrender our common one."[119] This teacher was surrendered and exceptional.

Still not sure what this surrendered teaching looks like? Matthew 6:31–33 says, "So do not worry saying, 'What shall we eat?' or 'What shall we drink?' or 'What shall we wear?' For the pagans run after all these things, and your heavenly Father knows that you need them. But seek first his kingdom and his righteousness, and all these things will be given to you as well." *Seek* the Lord—seek to *know* Him.

Read John 14: 23–27.

It is only by being acquainted with Christ Jesus and knowing His Word that the Holy Spirit can remind you how Jesus would respond in a situation. How can you have a relationship with someone if you never spend time with them? How much more important is it to spend time with Jesus in Bible reading, Bible study, prayer, meditation, and devotionals? This relationship will affect all our relationships.

In 1 Peter 2:9, it declares, "But you are a chosen people, a royal priesthood, a holy nation, a people belonging to God, that you may declare the praises of him who called you out of darkness into his wonderful light." You are chosen—CALLED—into God's service to reach out to others. Those who are called have common characteristics and focus:

Commitment—They have made a COMMITMENT to give the reins of their lives to God.

Have Faith—HOLD ON to the promises of Christ.

Relationship—They have a *two-way* RELATIONSHIP with the living God

Imitate—They strive to IMITATE Christ through knowledge of His Word.

Spirit—The HOLY SPIRIT is at work in their lives as evidenced by the fruits of the Spirit.

Transformation—TRANSFORMATION will occur. If you are focusing on CHRIST, if you are focusing on all these things, transformation into the "royal priesthood" will occur naturally and joyfully through no effort of your own. It will be a gift from God.

---

[118] Young, Sarah. *Jesus Calling*, p. 149.
[119] Lucado, Max. *Cure for the Common Life*, p. 86.

The disciples were ordinary men, no better and no worse than any of us. But when their lives became focused on CHRIST, they were transformed into apostles and saints. Acts 4:13 reads, "When … [the Council of Jewish leaders] saw the courage of Peter and John and realized that they were unschooled, ordinary men, they were astonished and they took note that these men had been with Jesus."

Teaching is not a particularly prestigious calling, nor is it one that is financially rewarding, but in the end, our legacy will not be how rich we are; our legacy will be how we have enriched the lives of others. Each of us has a personal and nontransferable mission.

We are called to have a focused relationship with Christ so that Christ's light reflected through us will cause our world to have hope and to know that Christ is alive and that we have, indeed, been with Jesus. "The main thing about Christianity is not the work we do, but the relationship we maintain and the atmosphere produced by that relationship. That is all God asks us to look after."[120] Just keep the main thing the main thing.

Before you change professions, try this:
change your attitude toward your profession.[121]

—Max Lucado

How is God using this lesson to equip you? Record meaningful statements, ideas, and scriptures you may want to remember and use as He equips you for the task for which His is calling you.

_____

_____

_____

_____

_____

_____

_____

---

[120] Chambers, Oswald. *My Utmost for His Highest,* August 4 reading.
[121] Ibid., p. 96.

Day 5
EQUIPPED TO FOLLOW THE CALL

MISSION POSSIBLE

"*L*IFE SHOULD *NOT* BE A journey to the grave with the intention of arriving safely in an attractive and well preserved body, but rather to skid in sideways, chocolate in one hand, body thoroughly used up, totally worn out, and screaming '*WOOHOO! What a ride!*'"[122] Now that's abundant life.

When you think of "abundant life," what comes to your mind? Does it mean having an abundance of things? Is it owning the newest state-of-the-art electronic gadgetry? Or the latest fashions? Is it being able to afford anything your heart desires? Does it mean living a long life? Does it mean constant "busyness"? Jesus said, "I came that they may have life, and have it abundantly."[123] Other translations denote a "fullness of life"—"that they may have life, and have it to the full."[124]

What does a "full" or "abundant" life look like? The apostle Paul, who really could be the role model for the beginning quote, gave the Colossians some "Rules for Holy Living" in Colossians 3:12–17.

- *Read Colossians 3:12–17*, and list some of Paul's major points.

  _____

  _____

  _____

Does some of Paul's litany for holy living sound familiar? In this passage, Paul rattled off five of the nine Fruits of the Spirit (kindness, gentleness, patience, love, and peace).[125] To these virtues, he added compassion, an "action version" of kindness, gentleness, and goodness. Paul also instructed us to have humility and to "bear with" and to forgive one another.

- What does "bearing with" others mean to you?

  _____

  _____

  _____

---

[122] Beam, Christy. Miracles from Heaven: A Little Girl, Her Journey to Heaven, and Her Amazing Story of Healing.
[123] John 10:10, Revised Standard Version.
[124] John 10:10, NIV.
[125] Galatians 6:22–23.

Remember the "dos" and "don'ts" of love in 1 Corinthians 13? Besides being patient and kind, we are taught in the Colossians scripture to be humble (do not envy, boast, be rude, or proud). Also, we are coached to bear with one another (don't be easily angered, don't be self-seeking, don't be happy about injustice but rejoice when truth wins out)[126] and to forgive (keep no record of wrongs). In Colossians 3:14, Paul said, "And over all these virtues put on love, which binds them all together in perfect unity (Love "always protects, always trusts, always hopes, always perseveres. Love never fails.").[127]

In Colossians 3:15, we are to "let the peace of Christ rule in [our] hearts" and "be thankful." Do you recollect Paul's "anxiety-free recipe"? "Rejoice in the Lord always. I will say it again: Rejoice! … Do not be anxious about anything, but in everything, by prayer and petition, with thanksgiving, present your requests to God. And the peace of God, which [is far beyond] all understanding, will guard your hearts and your minds in Christ Jesus" (Philippians 4:4–7). Can you visualize this? When we are purposefully looking to Jesus and willfully aligned with Him, God's peace will *guard* our hearts and minds! If we think we are in control of our lives, then there is very good cause for anxiety, but if we've gratefully given Jesus the steering wheel of our life, then our heart and mind can be at peace.

Do you see how the "Word of Christ can dwell in you richly" (Colossians 3:16)? Your example will teach and influence others as you, in gratitude and love, honor Jesus and glorify God in all you do. "Discipleship is … learning to give Jesus Christ total access to your life so He will live His life through you … When others watch you face a crisis, do they see the risen Lord responding? … There is a great difference between 'living the Christian life' and allowing Christ to live His life through you."[128]

There is one final word of scripture to equip us for daily battle—the armor of God. *Read Ephesians 6:10–17.*

Were you a bit surprised by Paul's discourse of the evil we come up against in our world? He made it clear in verse 12 that "our struggle is not against flesh and blood" or against the people we come in contact with daily. Perhaps that is why he says we must "bear with each other and forgive whatever grievances [we] may have against one another."[129] We live in a fallen world, where sin and evil are on the prowl, ready to pounce on us and use us to pounce on others and use them. In preparation for spiritual battle, Paul admonishes us to be strong in Him and to put on God's armor so we will be able to stand firm in Him and resist the onslaught of evil.

The Armor of God: Belt of _____

                                    Breastplate of _____

                                    Sandals of _____

                                    Shield of _____

                                    Helmet of _____

                                    Sword of _____

---

[126] 1 Corinthians 13:6, Living Bible.
[127] 1 Corinthians 13:7–8.
[128] Blackaby, Henry and Richard. *Experiencing God Day by Day*, p. 20.
[129] Colossians 3:13.

The first item a soldier would put on in readiness for battle is a strong belt, which would gird up his tunic and provide a secure place for his sword to hang. For Paul, the belt was a sign of commitment; the soldier, in truth, *is* dressing and preparing for battle.

Since we are *made right* before God through the blood of Jesus, God provides us with a breastplate of righteousness. In Paul's culture, thinking was associated with the heart, and the bowels were associated with feelings and "gut-wrenching" emotions.[130] We are prey to arrows of lies and deceit and destructive emotions without protection. We must put on the breastplate of righteousness intentionally and purposefully by continually moving toward God and seeking His point of view. Living a righteous life is a matter of daily choices that either keep us aligned with God and protected or choices that allow us to drift away and be vulnerable.

Since Adam's sin, man has been at war with God, and over and over, Paul preached that keeping Jewish law alone would not make us right with God. But Christ's sacrifice on the cross changed all that: "We have peace with God through our Lord Jesus Christ."[131] Therefore, we can stand firm and surefooted and ready and shod in knowledge and belief of the Gospel of Peace.

Paul warns us in verse 16 to "take up the shield of faith, with which you can extinguish all the flaming arrows of the evil one." This is an especially important piece of equipment in today's world. In ancient times, one might be confronted by information from and opinions of others, even a crowd of people, or perhaps an army might influence one's thinking. Today, however, we literally hold the world in the palm of our hand. Information, propaganda, deceit, and truth come streaming in from remote corners of the earth, and we are completely bombarded with data. In our world, choices are data-driven. Schools and companies are data-driven, but faith is not driven by the world's input. Many, many times believers are called to have faith and trust when data is to the contrary. "Wisdom is not what you know about the world but how well you know God,"[132] so keep up that shield of faith.

Think about the "helmet of salvation" in verse 17. We're covered. If the world wants to take us down, we're covered. Jesus said, "I tell you the truth, he who believes has everlasting life."[133] "Threaten me with heaven, that's all they can do."[134] Be confident in your salvation.

In that same verse it says we must take up "the sword of the Spirit, which is the word of God." This piece of equipment is the only offensive weapon we have. To be able to use the sword of the Spirit takes practice. We have the weapon in our hands that will bring us victory—the weapon that can slay the evil you encounter. If doctors practice medicine, then surely a believer must practice in God's Word. You have been practicing during this Bible study. Practice until you make the sword of the Spirit an extension of your arm, a part of who you are.

Finally, verse 18 tells us to "pray in the Spirit on all occasions with all kinds of prayers and requests." In other words, put on all the armor and then keep in constant communication with the Commander, Who assures us of victory. Have you checked the back of the book? He wins.

---

130 http://www.gty.org/Resources/Sermons/1956. Sermon by John Macarthur.

131 Romans 5:1.

132 Blackaby, Henry and Richard. *Experiencing God Day by Day*, p. 96. April 1.

133 John 6:47.

134 Grant, Amy. Track 14 "Threaten Me with Heaven," *How Mercy Looks from Here* CD.

That's called hope, "and hope does not disappoint us, because God has poured out his love into our hearts by the Holy Spirit, whom he has given us."[135]

"From the perspective of the Bible, hope is not simply a feeling or a mood or a rhetorical flourish. Hope is the very dynamic of history. Hope is the engine of change. Hope is the energy to transformation. Hope is the door from one reality to another … Hope is believing in spite of the evidence and watching the evidence change."[136]

We have journeyed through the centuries together. We have rubbed elbows with people just like us: people who laughed and cried, who got scared and angry; people who celebrated and mourned, who got frustrated and tired; and people who nursed hope by a spark of faith despite evidence to the contrary.

We walked for a while with Moses, David, Esther, and Paul. We saw how God called each of them in and through their ridiculous circumstances and how He girded and guided them as He equipped them.

We have sat at the knee of the Master Teacher who loves us and longs for us to follow His example and teachings, so through our teaching and example, others might grow toward Him as well. "Let your gentleness be evident to all. The Lord is near."

We are at the end of our journey together, but our journey is far from finished. *You*—in your home, in your job, in your church, in your exact circumstances, at this precise time in your life—are *called*. "Therefore as God's chosen, holy and dearly loved" you will be *equipped* for whatever lies ahead. *woohoo! What a ride!*

How is God using this lesson to equip you? Record meaningful statements, ideas, and scriptures you may want to remember and use as He equips you for the task for which He is calling you.

_____

_____

_____

_____

_____

_____

_____

---

[135] Romans 5:5.

[136] Wallis, Jim. *Journeying through the Days 2013.* March 1, 2.

GROUP QUESTIONS FOR YOU ARE CALLED

- We expect our students to be receptive and attentive. If we are to be equipped, that's what God expects of us. Discuss ways we can be more receptive/repentant and attentive to God's path for us. It takes a pinch of salt to make something more palatable. How might we be "pinched" into this call?

- Share with the group any unpleasant task that has/could become an opportunity to practice the presence of God.

- Share with the group if you have a reminder or trigger to help you watch for blessings during the day.

- Thy Rod and Staff Development Plan is designed to be done at the beginning of the school year or semester, while the Daily Rod and Staff Plan is to be a daily tithe. If your planning time is sixty minutes, a 10 percent tithe of this time is six minutes. Is this a good use of your time? Why?

- Max Lucado asks, "What if everyone worked with God in mind? Suppose no one worked to satisfy self or please the bottom line but everyone worked to please God." Could this mindset work in your school, classroom, or workplace?

- In teaching and in any job, you must learn to "bear with others." Discuss how this would look in your workplace.

- The sword of the Spirit is our only offensive weapon in the armor of God. Discuss how you can employ this weapon more skillfully.

Would you dare to believe

that God, who called you to Himself and equipped you with His Spirit,

could work mightily through you?

Have you made the connection

between the time and place in which you live and God's call upon you?

World events never catch God by surprise.

He placed you precisely where you are for a purpose …

Are you letting God use you

to make a difference in your generation?[137]

---

[137] Blackaby, Henry and Richard. *Experiencing God Day by Day*, p. 4. January 3.

Proceeds from the use and sale of *Called and Equipped* will go to

Brookwood in Georgetown,

a God-centered work and residential community

for adults with special needs.

Printed in the United States
by Baker & Taylor Publisher Services